A Nomad Called Thief

A Nomad Called Thief

REFLECTIONS ON ADIVASI SILENCE

G.N. Devy

Orient BlackSwan

A NOMAD CALLED THIEF

ORIENT BLACKSWAN PRIVATE LIMITED

Registered Office
3-6-752 Himayatnagar, Hyderabad 500 029, Telangana, India
e-mail: centraloffice@orientblackswan.com

Other Offices
Bengaluru, Chennai, Guwahati, Hyderabad, Kolkata,
Mumbai, New Delhi, Noida, Patna, Visakhapatnam

First Published 2006
Reprinted 2021

032978

ISBN 978-81-250-3021-8

Typeset in 12/15 pt. New Century Schoolbook

Typeset by
Bukprint
Delhi

Printed in India at
Yash Printographics
Noida

Published by
3-6-752 Himayatnagar, Hyderabad 500 029, Telangana, India
e-mail: info@orientblackswan.com

To
Mahasweta Devi
who brought me to the nomads

Acknowledgements

The texts brought together here have been published in various shorter forms in segments, in little magazines, journals, newspapers. Most of them have appeared in revised, curtailed or enlarged form more than once. These pieces are brought together here as, I suppose, together they give a better picture of my political and intellectual concerns, and more importantly, present the articles of my faith.

It is difficult for me to name the first place of publication of these essays with any great precision. For they have been written, rewritten, enlarged, abridged, reproduced, mixed, edited, and have appeared in print in all these versions. Besides, the statements in these essays have been used by the collective of my colleagues engaged in the adivasi movement focused round the Tejgadh experiment; to that extent this work is now more in the mode of an oral text.

However, based on my memory, I would like to gratefully acknowledge *The Hindu, The Times of India, India International Centre Quarterly, Seminar*, and *Budhan*, among publications, and Penguin India and Bhasha Publications, among publishers, for carrying previous versions of these writings.

I would like to thank Sarah Boltwalla and Kavita Patel for rendering into English my work from Gujarati. Sarah Boltwalla persuaded me that the Gujarati booklet *Vikas Vichar* was worth rendering into English, and, together with Kavita Patel, produced the English version 'Development', which is included here. I would like to thank Sonal Baxi for documenting and producing a readable transcript of the symposium on 'Adivasi Knowledge and Aphasia.'

For the tremendous encouragement given by Orient Longman and its editor Vidya Rao, I wish to thank them.

G.N. Devy

Contents

1

The Incomplete Blood Cell

I

Several images of village India have been in circulation over the last two centuries. In one set of images, the essential Indian village has herds of cows returning home at sundown, kicking dust into a reddened sky that reflects the glory of the large wheel of the sun. In the background are tiny temples, and thatched houses where oil lamps are being lit. Children, who have been playing all day long in the fields and along the river, say prayers, have meals and then slide into sleep listening to *kathas* and tales. After sunset and at night, ghosts hang around the huge trees of *vat*, *imali*, and *pimpal*, and the village gods and deities protect crops and the sleeping humans from evil spirits. Early in the morning the cock crows to herald the new day. Seasons flow uninterruptedly.

In another image, the village is an area of darkness, without schools, hospitals, roads, drinking water or hygiene, infested with mosquitoes, flies and snakes, without adequate nutrition or food supplies, and completely ignorant of the great advancements made by the rest of the country and the world in the areas of technology, science, medicine and communication.

Between the tranquil and the mute imagery of the Indian village are those other images which portray it as an economic bulwark, a laboratory in which the Green Revolution was worked out, the arena for caste-wars, the producer of an ever-increasing population, the real political-mass balancing power structure and even merely as the latest 'market'.

Perhaps all these images are at once valid, perhaps none of them is capable of being sufficiently convincing. The reason for this perpetual indeterminacy of the essential Indian village is that the variety is of such extraordinary magnitude that there can never be any single image of an Indian village that will hold true for the entirety of rural India.

In Kerala and Goa the divide between village and city is almost indistinct, whereas in Maharashtra and Gujarat the difference is quite dramatic. The agricultural villages in the plains have an architectural composition, which the adivasis in the forests and hills will not even be able to identify as a village. The nomads live in *tandas*, while in some parts of Andhra Pradesh and Karnataka houses are built of solid stone. The demographic composition too varies between the composite and ethnically pure. The northeastern states have villages completely cut off from the national political processes and social turmoil. A Punjab village might be many times more prosperous than even the state capitals of some Union Territories. There can be no single homogenous image of the village valid for the entire country.

And yet, it cannot be denied that what is perceived in different times and different locations, as 'India' is far more prominently present in Indian villages. Perhaps with all their diversity, all their differences, the half million villages of India continue to keep together the amorphous glory called Indian culture. That village India continues to represent Indian traditions is quite a miracle considering how heavily the entire process of economic modernisation is inclined in favour of non-rural India. At present nearly 40 per cent of India's population lives in cities and towns and invariably all decision-making mechanisms are controlled and manipulated by this powerful segment of Indian society.

There is something to be said in favour of the innate dynamism and resilience of rural India, which has traditionally learnt not only to survive but also how to renew the sources of its being. This wisdom comes from the accumulation of historical experience, of mediating between nature and power. The striking poise and the grace of village men and women, which is a result of the dignity acquired through labour and self-reliance, is evident in any part of India.

II

A village scene comes back to my memory.

This is about the time India became independent. It is winter. Tinkling bells surprise the dusty roads. Music vibrates in the darkness. The village wakes up. As doors open, people see a thin man, his headgear adorned with peacock feathers. Sometimes, the man has on his chest a metal-like standard bearing the emblem of the forest goddess. He is Vasudeva, the goddess is Vaghjai. Where she lives is as much unknown as where he lives. But their early morning visitation unfailingly punctuates the village calendar of seasons. In the evening, the riverbank is crowded with saffron. People come, from where no one knows, to perform *kirtana*. They sing till night descends. In the last months of winter, by January, these people are gone. The elders tell the children that they continue the pilgrimage, that during the pilgrimage their next halt will be at Vaghjai. Perhaps the Vasudeva will speak to them of stories heard a long time ago. The forest, thus, visits the village.

A dam had been built on the river in the early thirties. At a distance of hundreds of miles the Tatas had established a power generation centre. Prime Minister Nehru, whom the children liked very much, had said that electricity was the new lifeline for the new nation. And so electricity was generated at this dam too. But in the dam there was a lot of silting. In the late fifties, floods became recurrent. On the surface of the current, the amount of driftwood increased every year. It floated on the water, like the villages going off to the cities in search of new dreams, walking the state highways. Somewhere in the forest on the hills, the woods were losing their roots. The trees were being cut. As the driftwood increased in frequency and variety, the Vasudeva stopped coming to the village.

Inside a house, a steel wire hung by a peg. It was the solitary file; all papers, documents had to be hung by it, pierced like earlobes. At the bottom of that file of papers, about to disintegrate into powder, there hung a license issued by the British Collector. It gave the bearer the leave to purchase *beheda* from the forest guard—a herbal soap, worth six annas and four paise. The six annas grew in volume through the years of the colonial rule and became twenty truckloads by the time Mehboob Khan launched his celebrated *Mother India*, a movie that showed in some Bombay theatre for over a hundred weeks. No longer were the forest nuts used as herbal soap; they were sold to a rexine-manufacturing company to produce synthetic dyes. And now the forests were apparent on the surface coating of the school bags used all over the country by the children who adored the Prime Minister.

During the mid-sixties, there was widespread concern about the dwindling of forests. Everywhere along the highways one saw new plantations of eucalyptus. This was the time for the Green Revolution, for turning wasteland into cultivable land. The farm was foregrounded, the forest was forgotten. Some two decades later, the forest-dweller started surfacing unexpectedly on the national television. He usually came there in the month of January, to celebrate the country's nationhood, almost as if the Vasudeva who had walked away in the fifties had returned, much younger, more colourful and far more primitive. The forest was gone from the consciousness of the people. 'Forest-dweller' was an unused word in the dictionary of India's culture.

The useless and the unused are always a problem for history. They invariably return, disturb an established order and pose uncomfortable questions. The forest-dweller had done it once before in Sudraka's *Mrichchhakatika*. There, a wholesale rebellion is seen brewing in the forest; a challenge to all established orthodoxies is being articulated. The forest has a discourse of a charged silence. The political idiom of the forest-dweller is always abrupt. It understands relations and loyalties but no authority. This idiom suddenly acquires a strange energy and finds a voice.

III

From the time I started working with the adivasis, I have never ceased to learn from them. My first surprise was to discover that adivasis have no castes, that all persons in a given tribe are treated as equal in birth and death. The next was that they have no religion. This is not to say that they have no concept of the divine or the supernatural. In fact, they treat a large part of the realm of the physical as charged with the supernatural. There is an appropriate prayerfulness towards things material. But adivasis have not allowed their need to worship to grow into a basis for nationalism or for waging wars.

It is generally believed that they have a religion, which can be termed animistic. But that is not quite correct. Not all trees and plants or all hills and rivers, or all beasts and birds are sacred for them. There are clearly defined spaces and moments for the sacred. An example is the Rathwa tribe's Babo Pithoro. This god, spirit or ancestor, is depicted in the form of a large painting inside a Rathwa house. During the ritual of creating the painting and ordaining it as a sacred presence, the Rathwas observe certain rules of pollution. After the ritual is over, it survives as any other wall surface, allowing nails and pegs to go in, wall clocks and other things to hang on it. In other words the adivasi religion allows faith but does not imprison the mind.

When one looks at the adivasis, what stands out most is the powerful presence of the adivasi body. There is something fascinating about it. It is not just the absence of obesity, or the natural grace and charm with which an adivasi man or woman conducts himself or herself. There is something more to it, and it is the adivasi attitude to the human body. They do not look at the human body as cursed with mortality. They look to it as made of imperishable material towards which they have a great responsibility. So one finds that washing the body regularly, at least twice every day, decorating it with ornaments appropriate to the occasion and the hour of the day as defined by convention, celebrating its worldly transitions through song and dance, all these give the adivasi the utmost sense of satisfaction. The kind of joy that a Japanese gets in perfecting technology, a German in being dreadfully punctual, an American in dreaming big ideas, is the same joy that an Indian adivasi gets in keeping the body in a state worthy of adoration.

Acquisition is not a passion with the adivasis. Money and possession of land or cattle do not interest them beyond a point. Therefore, their work is not directed exclusively to the creation of wealth. Since wealth is not the only logical result of work, they do not exploit other people's work. They contribute work very generously for community welfare. All of them work together when a house is to be built for any family. Often they contribute labour to cultivate the land of a person who is ill or away from the village. They do not like to purchase labour in order to enslave others. And they do not like to become slaves themselves. They work in order to survive, not survive in order to work. As such, adivasis have succeeded in creating an extraordinary amount of leisure time, which is used for rest, dance, song, and the creation of small but beautiful objects of daily use that we invariably mistake for adivasi craft.

They are acutely sensitive to the law of the community but are totally unconcerned even bored with all other kinds of laws and regulations. That is why, when a murder takes place in an adivasi community, the offender loses no time in presenting himself to the police, confessing his crime in the courtroom and going through his years of interrment in our jails. In his heart, he finds the indignity and suffering involved in all this completely irrelevant to his being. But when the community panchayat takes up an issue as small as the insult of the in-laws, an adivasi will haggle over it, argue it out most vehemently, and even be prepared to give his life to save his honour.

Of all the things I have learnt about the adivasis, the most important is that we know very little about them. The people we are trying to civilise are far more civilised than us. As a matter of fact, we should be learning from them, rather than teaching them. Sadly, for quite some time we have been mindlessly destroying this great civilisation.

Here is a random list of what we have given the adivasis: Forest Acts depriving them of their livelihood; a Criminal Tribes Act and a Habitual Offenders Act; taxes and the tax collectors; alien languages for education; chemical fertilisers; a severe penal code; the compulsion to subscribe to a religion and to enter it in their birth certificates; existence as bonded labour; forest guards and private moneylenders; mosquitoes and malaria; naxalites and ideological war-groups; the Greyhound Police Academy; a schedule of their identity defined from outside; and perpetual contempt.

IV

It is a dark night, like a slate without a chalk mark. I wait, thinking about the wild animals that might be moving about in the darkness. My companions can be identified only when they speak, as if they exist only as formless, bodiless voices. These disembodied voices, these *shabdabrahman*, are the Rathwa adivasis, my companions. They have brought me to this lonely place on the outskirts of Tejgadh to witness a ritual procession. Unlike me, they are not tense. They know the exact timing and movements of the procession. 'It has started', they say, 'it is now moving. It is crossing the stream.' I don't see any of this. How can they? They tell me that they can hear the drumbeats. When they say this, I think I too can almost hear a drum, faint and distant like one's heartbeats. Then the drum is a little more audible. 'Now the womenfolk have joined the procession,' they say. They explain that the drums can convey about twenty-four types of signals. I try to decipher one beat from another, try to fathom the mysterious language, but without much success. Finally, from nowhere in the darkness, dots of wavering lights appear, a long distance from where we are. They are lanterns.

By now, I have stopped thinking about reptiles and tigers. Suddenly my mind recalls William Blake. When he wrote about the tiger burning bright, did he have an experience of this kind? Now the lanterns have grown brighter, they're swinging amorously. The drums have become drunken. I can now see the procession clearly.

It draws closer, pulls us towards the human stream. We move in its direction. I do not remember how far we walk. The procession carries everyone along with it, like a sleepy infant in its mother's arms. It is enveloped by drumbeats on all sides. Beautiful adivasi men and women are in it, singing songs of desire. These songs are in their blood carried from generation to generation.

The men, women and children are dressed in their most colourful costumes, jewellery and cosmetics, but they are neither vain nor narcissistic. They are more like devotees. Their faces, lit up by the lanterns, reflect holiness. The whole procession is a moving prayer, a silent stream flowing along for a communion with the larger ocean. The procession halts and I can see an arch made of green leaves and flowers, mostly marigold. The flowers look brighter in the dim light. Under the arch stand a man and a woman, and before them, a little child. This is a girl, perhaps two or three years old. She is radiant with the glow of good health and the love of her parents.

From the darkness appear more people. One of the men holds a large pile of marigold garlands. Another, older, is the *poojara*, the priest. In the darkness, these look like the images appearing on the negative of a photographic film. Even before I can take in all this, I hear a strange sound, not quite hissing, not quite moaning. I look in its direction and notice that a young man who was a part of the procession by my side is possessed. The people have formed a neat semicircle, framing an open space for the possessed.

The possessed man occupies this space, weaving from one end to the other unsteadily, like a nightmare unfolding in the unconscious. The *poojara* asks him some questions and identifies the spirit that has possessed his body so authoritatively. A garland is chosen for him and the little girl is asked to throw it round his neck. With the touch of the marigold, the spirit leaves the body, and the man returns to it - now standing in the semicircle and surrounded by the entranced people. Another spirit enters another body. The drums, which have not ceased to beat even for a moment, change their rhythm.

This time, the *poojara* selects a different kind of garland—for this one is another spirit. The girl once again manages to get it round the neck of the possessed man. He returns to the entranced crowd. One after another, spirits claim bodies, and bodies claim the space of the unconscious. One after another, the spirits are gratified and propitiated by the marigold garlands flying out of the little girl's hands. The trance thickens as the drums pierce through the darkness enticingly.

I have no idea how long I will watch this dialogue between the spirit and the body. My companions ask me to step into the space reserved for the possessed. I do so, blankly. They bring me closer to the girl. The *poojara* selects a different kind of garland for me. I lower my head and bend towards the girl. She offers the garland to me. I ask her name. She looks at me with eyes wide as the horizon, and answers with the confidence only innocent children have.

She is Urmila. I detect in those eyes a kind of fear, far more primitive than my fear of reptiles and tigers in dark forests. I am, as it were, her dark forest. I carry home with me the momentary revelation of truth and innocent wisdom like the ashes of a civilisation.

On the way back, my companions tell me that this has been a thanksgiving ritual. Some weeks ago, a cobra had entered Urmila's house and crawled up her body, but had not harmed her. It had then slithered out of the house. Urmila's parents wanted to thank the gods for entering into a dialogue with their daughter in the form of *naga-dada*, the cobra. The possessed men and women were these gods. Each god had to be thanked by offering a special type of garland.

I look at the garland in my hand. Which one of the gods am I? I remember that piercing dot of fear in her eyes as I spoke to Urmila. She can play with a cobra but cannot bear to see a citydweller like me. Her elders may pretend to be hospitable to me. They may pretend to include me in their prayers and rituals. But for them, as for her, I am an alien, someone who must be instinctively distrusted. The adivasi does not normally speak to city people not because he has nothing to say, but perhaps because what he wants to say to us is alarming.

Keats' 'Ode to a Grecian Urn' depicts an ancient procession, somewhat like the one I have just seen. His poem ends with the oft-quoted enigmatic sentence, 'Beauty is truth, truth beauty. That is all ye need to know'.

We know the beauty of the adivasis; but we do not know the truth about them. It lies far beyond the realm of the verbal. It rests somewhere in the darkness of the jungle. In a state of trance, and possessed by strange spirits, it surfaces occasionally. There is no entry into that world for us with our literal minds. One can enter it only through the path of faith, by accepting ritual, superstition and conventions on their own terms. It is only then that we may be able to make a beginning towards understanding adivasis. The task is as difficult as measuring the irrational by using rational parameters. The rift between the two civilisations is very wide. Or, perhaps, the adivasis of our country are the unconscious region of our civilisation?

V

The terms 'caste' and 'tribe' have stuck to Indian society ever since the Portuguese travel writers and missionaries used these terms to describe the vast variety of ethnic and occupational groups and sects of the Indian subcontinent, These terms have become much like long-worn masks that start acquiring real personality. The result is that today, no Indian describes Indian society without taking recourse to the categories 'caste' and 'tribe'. In the initial period of India's contact with western nations the two terms were used as synonyms, any difference between them lay only in the social status of the groups they described. In his discussion of the caste system, Louis Dumont tells us that almost till the end of the eighteenth century, 'caste' was used for the socially privileged groups as against 'tribe', which was used for groups lower in the social hierarchy. The colonial rulers finally shattered the synonymy through a legal intervention when an official list of communities was prepared by them (in 1872) as the list of Indian tribes. Since then the 'tribes' are perceived as a distinct segment of Indian society.

History has indeed been extremely unkind to the adivasi people in India. None of their brave fights against the British has ever been treated as part of the 'national' struggle for freedom. From the Bihar uprising of 1778 to Lakshman Naik's revolt in Orissa in 1942, the adivasis of India repeatedly rebelled against the British in the Northeast, Bengal, Bihar, Madhya Pradesh, Maharashtra, Gujarat and Andhra Pradesh. In many of the rebellions, the adivasis could not be subdued by the might of the empire. The struggle was terminated only because the British acceded to their immediate demands, as in the case of the Bhil revolt of 1809 and the Naik revolt of 1838 in Gujarat.

But while the adivasis kept fighting in the hills and forests, the rest of India was being educated and 'civilised', and its self-cognition was mesmerised so totally, that, when Independence came, India started thinking of the adivasi people as the primitives who had been forever out of step with history. The plight of the Notified Tribes was even worse. The country did not wake up till August 1952 to the fact that their 'denotification' should have been announced on the midnight of our tryst with destiny. Similar to some half-dead bodies that remain trapped under the debris of an earthquake even after rescue operations are complete, tribes have remained trapped in the debris of colonial history which first marked them out as the most rebellious and then labelled them as the most primitive communities.

The truth, however, is that there is much in the adivasi way of life that the country needs to emulate. Adivasis do not rape their women, beat and abuse their children, exploit nature beyond satisfying minimum human needs, lend money at interest, burn widows, or segregate and stratify labour in terms of caste.

Looking back on the half-century of utter confusion and casualness of India's attitude to the adivasis, one wonders if there has been any difference at all between the adivasi situation during the colonial period and that in independent India. Obviously, one will point to the provision of special reservations for the Scheduled Tribes in education and in government jobs, reserved constituencies in Assemblies and the Parliament, the establishment of the Development sub-plans and a state sponsored corporation like Trifed. Indeed, these are some favourable signs of India's concern for the adivasi communities. However, the question is not just how effective they have been, but, and more pertinently, if there has been any vision of the adivasi past, present and future in the national policy.

Verrier Elwin, to whom we owe so much of the contemporary knowledge about adivasis, had advocated the principle of cautious and graded intervention in adivasi communities. Jawaharlal Nehru adopted his formula, known in his days as the Panchsheel, as the state policy for adivasis. He also effected the denotification of the communities branded as 'criminal tribes'. In Elwin's case, the policy of minimum intervention was the result of his deep involvement with and love for the adivasis. Translated in terms of state policy, it turned out to be mere tokenism. Under it the adivasis became an indispensable spectacle during the Republic Day parades and pageantry on display before foreign dignitaries. For the rest of the time, the adivasi could be whisked away, his lands acquired at will, the rivers and forest that nourished his life blocked and destroyed to build roads, dams, airports and film-cities. The adivasi population has been perceived by successive governments as a mass of people without their own will and wisdom. Besides, if and when untouchability is completely wiped out and the erstwhile unfortunate castes find some routes of upward social mobility, adivasis are expected to fill the gap and take the lowest position in the social hierarchy. Since traditionally most deposits of minerals lay in adivasi areas, and the locations of all big dams too were close to their habitations, a network of big industry has emerged in India all along the adivasi areas. The natural process of economic osmosis, therefore, has been attracting the adivasi work force — educationally ill-equipped as it is — to the industrial areas. Perhaps, the country seems to be eagerly waiting for the ninety million adivasis to lose their identity and 'assimilate' in the great Indian melting pot as the newfound lowest caste. The zest with which the debates about the exact religious denomination of adivasis are being carried out points to this great historical conspiracy of social engineering.

The debates really should have been not whether adivasis are, or ought to be, Hindus, Christians or Muslims, but rather, why most of them are afflicted with the sickle cell disease, why adivasi children drop out of the school system at an alarming rate, why the biodiversity conserved by them is on the decline everywhere, and how their land-alienation and indebtedness can be brought to an end. The central issue is whether the adivasis have any vision of their own progress and development, whether they have any voice of their own. When their voices are raised at all, they are heard as insurgents and are brutally smothered. The Constitution does not recognise even one of the eighty-odd languages of the adivasis, however major and ancient, as deserving of inclusion in the Schedule of languages. In such a situation, aphasia, or the loss of tongue, seems to be the fate of the adivasi language communities.

We have collectively, and without the consent of the adivasis, decided that there be national academies for the arts, craft and literature of caste-India, but no such provision is necessary for adivasi arts, craft and literature. A century and a half of deeply flawed education has taught us to ape the west in every respect. It has also taught us to leave the adivasis out as the apes of the great Indian society. And all that we have so far doled out in the name of adivasi policy is but an attempt at extermination of adivasi cultural traditions so that they remain without a voice, and merely make space for our progress, become our low-grade clones and provide us with cheap labour. In the process, we have forgotten that much that is valuable in Indian society, culture and heritage is of adivasi origin, that in fact the adivasi still has much with him that we stand to benefit by emulating. Rarely have we looked at the adivasi communities as leaders, who can reveal to us what civilisation is truly about.

Hence at the beginning of the new millennium we must open this question again and work towards formulating a comprehensive adivasi policy, which will help both the nation and the adivasi people. The four principles that we must follow while conceiving such a policy ought to be related to the recognition of the diversity of adivasi communities, their special educational needs, an utmost concern for their genetic mutations, and the recognition of the peculiar character of adivasi polity.

It is necessary to recognise that all adivasi communities are not alike, that they are products of different historical and social conditions and that they belong to four different language families and several different racial stocks and animistic moulds. Therefore, no uniform policy is ever likely to benefit all adivasi communities throughout the country. Next, if this huge work force has to be given special skills, which will improve their economic status, the existing formalities for educational advancement will have to be suspended, and a new kind of non-formal educational structure will have to be evolved. Thus special adivasi academies, which combine the merits of regular schools and the open universities, will have to be instituted. A National Adivasi Academy, which will regulate the education network, will have to be created for this purpose. Similarly, those adivasi communities, which have become victims of mutated gene diseases, such as the Korkus and the Bhils, will have to be provided with a special kind of health monitoring system so that the country does not quietly write off these as communities with defective genes. And finally, it is necessary to recognise that the adivasi polity be more closely regulated by the aesthetic pulse rather than an ethical drive, and, therefore the implementation of the adivasi self-governance provisions will have to go hand in hand with a special programme for encouraging adivasi arts, oral traditions and their unique skill in craft. If we fail to recognise this difference, which is vital to the social organisation of adivasi communities, and fail to respect it, we will end up creating bands of forced nomads who will only add to the urban chaos already overburdened with problems. Ultimately, what is good for the adivasis is also in the interest of the national common good.

However, the situation as it now prevails clearly indicates that these are but pious thoughts. The entire lot of denotified tribes has been left to the mercy of the crime-merchants. It is a routine experience for the men to die in police custody; the women experience being sold several times to several buyers. Neither the central government nor the states have made any concrete plans for a long-term upliftment programme. The situation is so alarming that in many states the governments do not have even the complete lists of the nomadic and denotified groups.

The political leadership in adivasi areas has been a victim of the party-system. When adivasi representatives get elected, they quickly get submerged in the main concerns of the party to which they belong. In any case, these parties have, at best, a nominal place for adivasi issues. On the other hand, when adivasi masses express their dissent, it is seen as an anti-state activity, resulting in an unnecessary burden on state funds at one end and a blatant violation of human rights at the other.

Those adivasis who have accepted facelessness as the only option for survival and have migrated to cities have yet to find a place even in the city slums. The slums too have their caste-structure; and adivasis do not easily fit into it. Their children remain without any education and add to the already swollen ranks of child labourers.

Colonialism has left many undesirable legacies for us to negotiate. But its impact on our self-perception has been among the most disastrous of those legacies. The categories of 'caste' and 'tribe' have coloured our vision of Indian society so much so that it seems unlikely that in the near future we will be able to recognise the people we call adivasis as other than 'adivasi'.

VI

The people of the Dhulia district in north Maharashtra are known as Pavaras; the name is derived from the Pavari language that they speak. They recount several versions of the genesis of their community but all the versions begin with memories of happiness before a great deluge forced them to move away from Pavagadh in Gujarat, some two hundred kilometres away. Every story of the genesis refers to place names such as Chhota Udaipur and Kanwat, places which do exist in Gujarat but which the Pavaras from Dhulia have not visited in recent times. Scattered over an area of several hundred kilometres in the Aravalli hills, the Pavaras carry within their collective memory an unwritten history of migration, perhaps forced on them three to four centuries ago.

To a casual visitor, a typical Pavara village appears as a portrait of pastoral bliss. Men and women cultivate the farms, and children go fishing in nearby streams with their homemade fishing nets. The houses are large, spacious and cool in summer. Illness among the young and old is rare and life expectancy is well above seventy. But a closer look at their life destroys this impression. The great Marathi poet Dilip Chitre was asked some two decades ago to prepare a documentary film on the life of the Pavaras. Sponsored by a cooperative sugar factory, the brief was to show the progress brought about by the spread of literacy among the Pavaras. Chitre began his work rather innocently; but frequent visits to the Pavara hills convinced him that what had to be projected as progress was really a decline from the high civilisational value of the Pavaras. Traditionally they used earthen jars to keep drinking water cool. Now the cooperative banks were prepared to advance them loans to purchase refrigerators, which in any case they did not need. The grinding stones in their houses were technically efficient as well as aesthetically sophisticated but the cooperative bakery now offered loaves of readymade white bread. Their economy was bound to ecology through the mahuda tree, used for nutrition as well as for making liquor. The beer brewed in Bangalore or Chandigarh now held more attraction. 'Progress' created desires and needs, which in no way added to the happiness of the Pavaras. Halfway through the production, Chitre decided to create a huge montage of images, mixing visuals of crushed sugar-cane and the happy faces of Pavara children. Towards the end of the montage the two images became inseparable. The sponsors did not like the poet's vision. The film production was halted and the footage was shelved. No one, not even Chitre, knows where the film is now.

But the march of progress continues. Subhash Pawra is a handsome young man from Akrani village near Dhadgaon. He is deeply concerned with the happiness of his community. When I visited the village, he showed me with great pride the school textbooks he teaches in the school. They were all in the Marathi language. He said, 'But the children must learn Marathi since they need jobs. They must also learn English.' However, when I told him that I was interested in the preservation of the Pavari language, he let his 'progressive' mask drop and agreed whole-heartedly that there was very little future for the Pavari language. He was quick to add that like the Pavagadh of his memory, which he had never visited, the children in his community may merely carry the name of their mother tongue in their memory without ever being able to speak or understand it. Well, which lump of sugar sold in the supermarket remembers the cane field from where it came?

A month after my visit to Akrani, Subhash travelled to Baroda to attend a workshop on adivasi literature. He had brought with him a number of Pavara stories, both pleasurable and painful. On meeting the other participants in the workshop drawn from different adivasi communities, it dawned on him that his was not the only community being pushed towards 'progress'. As his personal comment on this collective destiny of adivasi communities being crushed in the republic of India, he found out from me how to get to Pavagadh and made a sojourn to this centre of the Pavara universe before returning to his village. Subhash Pawra is probably the only Pavara to have made this journey into the past.

Pavagadh in Gujarat and Akrani in Dhulia, Maharashtra are separated by the deep flowing Narmada river. Massive dams are being built along its course. Some of the Pavaras from Aravalli hills have been displaced by the Narmada project. I met a group of displaced Pavaras in their rehabilitation colony near Vaghodia in Baroda district. They revealed that they had not brought with them their icons of worship. Nor has any shaman or priest accompanied them. They fancy that, in case of any 'emergency' in ritual or spiritual matters, they will go back to their original place in Dhulia. Little do they know that they are set on a journey of no return, that they must learn to live in the ugly tin sheds built for them by the Deputy Engineer Saheb and accept their godless existence as the new promised land.

Since they have no arts, no ritual, no mahuda trees left with them in this barren tin shed settlement, most of them have already been dreaming of migrating to cities like Baroda and Bharuch as construction workers. When the opulent houses in Baroda are built, these adivasis will end up in some nearby slum as the by-product of our progress. The sugar lumps and the crushed and twisted chaff will then be totally separated.

VII

The right to have a complete blood cell needs no defence in any country and at any time. It is the minimum expectation of any human being that the blood cells in his or her body should be like the blood cells of every other human being. But if, suddenly, the social conditions start making them incomplete and fragmented, it should be a cause for alarm to those who believe that human society has a goal higher than the exploitation of the vulnerable. Generally we are not aware that such a thing has happened or is happening in our own time. But visit Melghat in Maharashtra, for instance, to learn that this is just what is happening. The road to Melghat is not easy. Most people in Maharashtra do not know where it is, and what passes for a road here is not negotiable even if one were travelling in a jeep. The Amravati district is one of the most backward districts of Maharashtra. Since it is predominantly populated by adivasis, the government has found no good reason to develop it.

The adivasi community that lives in this area is known by the name 'Korku' which has by now come to be used as an insult by the Marathi speakers of the surrounding area. The Korkus were involved in a major development project in the last quarter of the nineteenth century. The railway company, laying tracks for the Surat-Howrah line, rounded them up to work as labourers. The Korkus had never been agriculturalists. Their values were not defined by a sedentary style of life. They were hunter-gatherers. The forest was their first and ultimate divinity. At the end of the railway line project, the Korku forest lay down as lifeless wooden sleepers carrying on its back the British soldiers and their supplies. The British were kind, of course. In exchange for the forest they gave the Korkus land for cultivation, which was however not exactly cultivable. Nor had the Korkus the skills to cultivate, or the centuries of wisdom that goes in exploiting land resources for creating surplus to support them. In a matter of four to five generations the Korkus found that the land given to them was not yielding enough to feed their hungry children. 'Malnutrition' is the word used in the diction of

WHO to describe the Korku situation. The Government of Maharashtra, too, came to know about their problem and found it advisable to appoint a committee of doctors to investigate whether the Korkus were not creating an unnecessary hue and cry. The doctors investigated the matter and concluded that it was, after all, entirely the fault of Korkus. If they carried the sickle-cell gene within them, how could the government be blamed for their early deaths? The doctors referred to the dictionaries of medical terms and said, 'This is how people with comma-shaped red blood-cells die.' Every school-going child reads in the textbook that sickle cell anaemia is a genetic disease, that this incomplete red blood cell collapses at the first instance of an external attack. And if one's body does not have a resistance mechanism within it, what else can it do but die early? The Government of Maharashtra said, 'If the Korku children die before attaining the fifteenth year of age, it is their parents who should be held responsible for passing on the genetic defect. If the Korkus are born genetically defective, what can India do?'

Or, if you live very far from Maharashtra and somewhere in the South, visit the Wynad district. You find the same story there. The characters are the same, only the plot changes. The adivasis of Wynad, too, have brought the story of genetic defect to bear upon India's development. If medical science says that sickle cell is an incurable disease, what can the government do but merely collect the figures of the numbers affected by it?

The statistics are frightening. For instance, approximately two million of the adivasis in Gujarat's total of seven million carry the sickle cell curse in their blood. It unnerves other people involved in the work of development. So, the government too, is cautious. We do not have the exact figures made public even today. It is only rumoured in official circles that the sickle cell is a typical adivasi disease. It is another thing that the category 'adivasi' is fictitious and was created as a social aberration by the British listing of communities in 1872. Never mention to the Public Health Department that the adivasis of India speak languages belonging to four different language families, that they are not a homogeneous group of blood relatives. Adivasi blood, after all, is not an asset of any national importance in India, whether it is the blood of adivasis or Denotified Communities, or of migrating adivasis. Therefore, how should it matter to anybody whether his or her blood cells are complete or incomplete?

I am sure that medical science on this issue is scientifically right. But I am not sure if it is absolutely right. Otherwise, completely unrelated adivasi groups could not have been the victims of the incomplete cell disease. It is perhaps possible that malnutrition for generations has imposed this condition of perpetual anaemia on them. I do not know if getting a square meal could be treated as a basic human right. Certainly, there seems to be a serious disagreement on this issue among the people who live in the economic capitals of the world. However, I think it should be possible for all human beings to recognise the right to having a complete cell as a basic human right. Merely leaving out nine crores of adivasi Indians as genetically defective will not be an act that can qualify for any kind of forgiveness.

Bengali writer Mahasweta Devi, who feels as agitated as I do about our insensitivity to adivasis, has written a story with a victim of sickle cell disease as the hero. In the conclusion of the story, she shows that the hero representing the Korkus, Kolis, Vasavas, Tadvis, Nayakdas and such other tribes enters the city of Bombay and is amazed to see that a thing called food exists there. He starts eating everything including the houses his ancestors built, the factories they worked in, and the train tracks they laid. I think Mahasweta Devi's vision is right. I think the right to eat it all should be recognised as the first biological right of the incomplete blood cell.

2

A Nomad Called Thief

I

The social category generally known as the Denotified and Nomadic Tribes of India covers a population of approximately six crores. Some of them are included in the list of Scheduled Castes, some others in the Schedule of Tribes, and quite a few in the category Other Backward Classes. But there are many of these tribes, which find place in none of the above. What is common to all these Denotified and Nomadic Tribes (DNTs) is the fate of being branded as 'born' criminals.

The story of the DNTs goes back to the early years of colonial rule. In those times, whoever opposed the British colonial expansion was perceived as a potential criminal. Particularly, if any attempt was made to oppose the colonial government with the use of arms, the charge of criminality was a certainty. In their list of criminal groups, the British included many of the wandering minstrels, fakirs, petty traders, rustic transporters and disbanded groups of soldiers. During the first half of the nineteenth century, the tribes of the northwest frontier were declared 'criminal tribes'. This category became increasingly open-ended, and by 1871 the British had prepared an official list of Criminal Tribes. An act to regulate criminal tribes was passed in that year. For instance, the Bhils who had fought the British rule in Khandesh and on the banks of Narmada were convicted under section 110 of the Indian Penal Code and were recognised as criminal tribes. The Criminal Tribes Act made provisions for establishing reformatory settlements where the 'criminal' adivasis could be kept in confinement and subjected to low paid work. They were required to report to the guard rooms several times every day, so that they did not escape the oppressive settlements.

By 1921, the CT Act was extended to cover numerous other tribes in the Madras Presidency, Hyderabad and Mysore. Thus, about the time that Indian politics saw the emergence of Mahatma Gandhi as the leader of the freedom struggle, Indian society mutely witnessed the emergence of a new class of people who were branded as born criminals.

Soon after Independence, the communities notified as criminal adivasis were denotified by the Government. This notification was followed by the substitution of a series of Acts, generally entitled 'Habitual Offenders Act' (HOA). The denotification and the passing of the HOAs should have ended the misery of the communities penalised under the CT Act. This however did not transpire, as the HOAs preserved most of the provisions of the former CT Act, except the premise implicit in it that an entire community could be 'born' criminal. But the police forces as well as the people in general had been taught to look upon the 'criminal tribes' as born criminals during colonial times and that attitude persisted and persists even today. One does not know if the police training academies in India still teach trainees that certain communities are habitually criminal. But the CT Act is very much a part of the syllabus leading to the discussion of crime-watch. The result is that every time there is a petty theft in a locality, the DNTs in the neighbourhood become the first suspects. The ratio between the arrests and the convictions of the DNTs needs to be analysed to see the extent of the harassment caused by the police to this most vulnerable and disadvantaged section of our society. The land possessed by the 'criminal' tribes was already alienated during colonial rule. After independence, various state governments have done little to restore their land to them. Schemes for economic uplift do not seem to have benefited them. The illiteracy rate amongst the DNTs is higher than among the Scheduled Castes or the Scheduled Tribes, malnutrition more frequent and provisions for education and health care almost negligible, since most of the DNTs have remained nomadic in habit. Above all, there is no end to the atrocities that the DNTs have to face.

Being illiterate and ignorant of the law of the land, the DNTs know very little about police procedures, and so they often get into difficult situations. The onus of proving innocence rests with them. I have known many among them who are scared to wear new clothes for fear of being arrested for theft. Therefore they soil their new clothes before using them. Lynched, hounded from village to village, starved of all civic amenities, deprived of the means of livelihood and gripped by the fear of police persecution, the DNTs of India are on the run. Freedom has still not reached them.

II

Budhan is just a name among thousands of names used in rural India. Budhan — a child born on Wednesday, the day of the planet Budha. There was one such Budhan in the Kheria Sabar community of West Bengal's Purulia district. He died in police custody in February 1998. That is when things changed. Budhan left behind him his widow Shamli and three children; but his death also created a movement for protection of the human rights of the Denotified Tribals of India. The credit for steering this movement goes to Mahasweta Devi. She has been working untiringly for the last two decades among the adivasis of Bengal, Bihar and other states, has established welfare centres and societies among them, written about them, fought for their rights, filed cases, advocated causes in their interest. Perhaps no one since the days of Verrier Elwin has displayed such deep empathy for the adivasis as she has.

When Budhan Sabar was killed, I happened to be at Midnapore attending a national seminar on Tribal Literature. Several tribal writers and activists travelled with me from Mumbai to Midnapore. All of us wanted to meet and hear Mahasweta Devi who was the main speaker of the seminar. One of these writer activists was

Laxman Gaikwad, whose phenomenal rise from anonymity to the status of a celebrity has been recorded in his moving autobiography *Uchalya* (for which he won the Sahitya Akademi Award). Our first meeting was brief; but we decided to meet again in Baroda on 14 March of that year, where Mahasweta Devi was to deliver the second Verrier Elwin lecture for the Bhasha Research and Publication Centre. Laxman Gaikwad too agreed to join us for the event. Many other writers and activists came to Baroda to attend the Elwin Lecture and to participate in a field trip I had organised that was to precede the lecture.

Mahasweta Devi's lecture was on 'Denotified Tribals Today'. It was well attended and highly applauded. After returning home, we talked through most of the night about our respective involvement with adivasis. The next day we visited the new training institute that Bhasha Centre is establishing at Tejgad. We continued our discussion throughout the night till the morning of 16 March. It was on that day that Mahasweta Devi and Laxman Gaikwad held a press conference in my office to announce the birth of DNT-RAG: The Denotified and Nomadic Tribals Rights Action Group. We prepared a statement, which was issued to newspapers and sent to a large number of activists throughout the country. It defended the basic human rights of the DNTs.

Two weeks later I was invited to deliver the keynote address at a seminar on the works of Mahasweta Devi by the university at Warangal in Andhra Pradesh. Mahasweta Devi herself was present. By then the Budhan Sabar case had been covered extensively by the Bengali press. There was rarely a day on which Mahasweta Devi did not speak with the utmost anxiety about the outcome of the court case that she had filed in favour of Shamli, Budhan's widow. We held a well-attended press conference at Hyderabad, and decided to travel to Mumbai to speak to the press there. It was here that we planned the future course of the new movement.

Since it was necessary to communicate with a large number of activists, volunteers and community-workers, and to keep them informed of all developments, we decided to produce a four-page newsletter. I thought *Budhan* would be an appropriate title. When

Mahasweta Devi saw the first printed copy, there were tears in her eyes - of anger, of sadness, of gratitude.

I could never keep to the four-page formula. There was so much to write about, to share with fellow workers, to report, that *Budhan* soon started looking like a regular journal. Four issues every month was a mammoth task; very soon the two editors - Gita Chauhan and I - decided that we could at best publish only six issues a year.

Something else happened in between. On 12 May, Mahasweta Devi and I travelled to Ahmedabad in search of the Chhara community. We had however, not much luck. We could barely get to the locality and look at the former settlement, where the Criminal Tribes used to be kept in soft confinement. The police supervised all our movements. However, some time later I did manage to get there again unobserved, meet some young people and establish at least a nominal communication with them. By the end of the month, video activist Nimmi Chauhan managed to film a video on the Chharas, which I showed to Mahasweta Devi and also other friends in Delhi.

In June we had the first public meeting of DNT-RAG in Chharanagar. At this meeting, the inhabitants asked us to start a public library which we did. In July the library was inaugurated by the Baroda-based painter Bhupen Khakhar. The library was named after Mansingh Chhara, himself a painter. In August we held a literary meeting in the very premises where the Chharas were kept in confinement prior to the denotification. Mahasweta Devi presided over the meeting, and Khakar, Kanji Patel and Bharat Naik read out from their Gujarati works. On that occasion young men and women surprised us by performing an extremely moving play - in the genre of a street play – on the theme of police atrocities on denotified communities. Therefore, when Chharanagar was chosen as the venue for the first national convention of the DNTs, it was decided that these talented young persons should be invited to perform before the national gathering.

In July, Justice Ruma Pal of the Calcutta High Court gave the historic judgment in the Budhan Sabar case and we carried the entire text of the judgment in the *Budhan* issue for that month.

When the national convention was held at Chharanagar on 31 August, the range of speakers was impressive: Justice D.K. Basu, Romila Thapar, Mahasweta Devi, Gayatri Chakravorty Spivak, Pradeep Kumar Roy, Laxman Gaikwad, Ratan Kodekar and Surekha Devi. After the speeches came the play. There was hardly anybody in the audience who did not feel profoundly moved to see the Chhara youths enacting the entire Budhan Sabar case. With what passion, with what ease do they act, these Chhara boys and girls! Some of them have their fathers, brothers, relatives in police custody and jails. There was very little in the play, which has not been a part of their daily lives.

Word of the convention and DNT-RAG went round. A few days, after the convention I was surprised to find a letter in my mail from Mallika Sarabhai, the celebrated artist-activist. She expressed her desire to perform for the DNT-RAG. I was not very certain whether she really meant this. So I stayed quiet for a few weeks. But, when there was an occasion to go to Ahmedabad, and particularly since Mahasweta Devi was to be with me and Surekha (my wife), I called Mallika. Her mother Mrinaliniben asked us for lunch at which we spoke to them about the DNTs and their problems. Two weeks later, I read an extremely well-written article on this meeting in *The Times of India*. It was by Mallika in her column 'View from the Bridge'.

The result of this meeting was that the Chharas were introduced to the Sarabhais and their Darpana Academy. On 17 November, *Budhan* was performed in the Darpana theatre. Mallika Sarabhai had invited judges, police officers and the theatre lovers of Ahmedabad to the performance. It was followed by a soul-searching discussion about the plight of the DNTs. The Chharas, for the first time since colonial incrimination, were treated humanely and given thoughtful consideration.

I wanted to see how a different audience would receive the play. So I invited it to Tejgadh, where it was performed on 28 November in an open ground before the villagers—which included a group of the Chamtha denotified community, children, adivasi women and a group of visiting students from the National Institute of Design, Ahmedabad. And it worked again–though very differently. The response was participatory; there was understanding rather than anger in the minds of the people who came to see the play on that cold evening.

The next day as I was walking in the village, I heard some children miming the actors, reproducing lines from the dialogues. These adivasi children who live several thousand miles away from Budhan Sabar's village will never know how this name has travelled to Tejgadh in western India. They did not know that some months ago Mahasweta Devi and Laxman Gaikwad had gone to Tejgadh thinking of starting a new movement. But they recognised the shades of experience that are a part of their daily life, which the Chharas had brought to them as a dramatic tale. Budhan had become a myth, a symbol of India's vast community of the vulnerable and victimised. A man, a name, and a symbol: Budhan. So do myths spring up and grow. And so do they carry within them such pain!

III

Until April 1998 I had only heard about the Chharas or read about them in local Gujarati newspapers. Moreover, the little I had heard or read did not encourage me to meet them, for it referred to them in very unflattering terms, ascribing to them criminal and anti-social tendencies. Therefore, when I decided to acquaint myself with the Chhara community of Gujarat after DNT-RAG was launched in March 1998, I was not surprised to find that the way to Chharanagar was laden with suspicion and contempt. Initially, I had asked a young painter friend to visit Chharanagar in Ahmedabad and obtain some basic details about the community. Chakradhar, the painter, reported that none of his friends in Ahmedabad were willing to take him to Chharanagar. Therefore, I decided to seek help from a former student of mine, who is now a Sessions Judge in Ahmedabad. She said that she could not go to Chharanagar herself or accompany me there since she has to judge many cases with the Chharas as the accused. However, she offered to call the

Commissioner of Police, who in turn offered to send a Police Inspector with me to Chharanagar.

Ahmedabad is normally hotter, dustier and more choked with smoke than Baroda. It was much more so on that day in April 1998 when Mahasweta Devi and I were taken to Chharanagar in a police jeep. There we spent half an hour at the police station listening to the official version of the criminality of the Chharas. When we requested a meeting with some members of the community, a few elders were called. They all looked and talked like police-informers. With them we went on a conducted tour through a narrow lane full of puddles and an overwhelming stench of country brew. During this tour we met a remarkable woman called Mrs Indira Jackson, a widow, maidservant or a housewife, perhaps. Pitch dark in complexion and with eyes that seemed to burn the beholder, she spoke in a thundering voice about her days at the settlement in Hubli, Karnataka. She was named Jackson because the officer in charge of the settlement was a Mr Jackson, and Indira because Jawaharlal Nehru who brought about the denotification of the settlement had a sweet little daughter called Indira.

She reminded me of the large-hearted and short tempered Wodder (or Wadar) women I had seen as a child, working in stone quarries in south Maharashtra. This Indira Jackson of Chharanagar was in the business of brewing liquor. While Mahasweta Devi in her Bengali Hindi, was conversing with Indira Jackson in her Kannada-Gujarati-Hindi, quite a crowd gathered around us. The police-escort had by now left. In the crowd I spotted a young man in a clean white shirt. He was Arvind Kodekar, an advocate. He told us that there were as many as sixty Chharas with law degrees, one Chhara girl with a diploma in fashion technology, some schoolteachers and numerous others with college education. But there were no jobs, 'Even when a Chhara has a first class degree he does not find employment. People distrust us. So finally everybody is compelled to get back to this ghetto.'

As we were leaving Chharanagar, Arvind mentioned that a scholar from Gujarat University had written an M.Phil dissertation on the Chharas. My attempts to get a photocopy of the work were not immediately successful but when I did get it, I found that the study ran on the following lines:

Chharas, the dissertation said, train their children, particularly girls, at a very young age to run liquor stocks, often smuggling them in balloons put inside their blouses. A Chhara who works as a clerk in some government office, carries his wife on his bicycle so that she can beg outside the office. Chharas were described as petty thieves. Exact amounts earned from these trades were mentioned. The dissertation also mentioned in its overview chapter the historical context of the Chhara ghetto.

I returned to Chharanagar a few days later and looked for Indira Jackson, but could not trace her. However, I found Arvind and explained to him that I had nothing to do with the police department and that I was a member of a Committee appointed by the National Human Rights Commission to study the problems of denotified communities. This time he was much friendlier than on the previous occasion. He introduced me to some other Chharas, all of whom were highly educated.

Two days later I requested Nimmi Chauhan of Drishti, Ahmedabad to film a video documentary on Chharanagar, which she prepared in a short time at considerable risk. I watched the video in Delhi together with Mahasweta Devi. The most striking part of it was an interview with advocate Ratan Kodekar. Ratan spoke with conviction and a deep commitment to the social transformation of the Chharas. He narrated with a wealth of detail how every innocent Chhara child is compelled to get into crime and how all attempts at finding other occupations are foiled by the police. He spoke so well that one thought he had graduated from an ivy-league university. On my return home, I telephoned Ratan and requested him to come immediately to Baroda for a meeting. He met me the next day and the story of a long struggle began, as if history had set the stage for it.

The British did not understand the communities that were non-sedentary. Therefore all nomadic communities became suspect in the eyes of the colonial British rulers. They drafted a unique piece of legislation in 1871 which they thought would tame the nomadic communities. This legislation was called the Criminal Tribes (CT) Act. The CT Act passed through a series of revisions till 1924. It provided for confiscation of land and other possessions and the forced internment of the so-called criminal tribes. Special areas for confining the 'criminals' were created. They were called settlements. Nearly two hundred nomadic communities were brought under the provisions of the CT Act. After Independence, the notification issued during the colonial regime was repealed. Therefore, these communities came to be known as denotified tribes. But the stigma attached to them persisted. The members of the public and the police continued to look upon them as criminals. The police in particular used this situation in an exploitative manner. The state governments or the central government offered little solace to the DNTs since they were distributed in the ST, SC and the OBC categories. The Chharanagar settlement is probably the largest of the settlements in Gujarat. Situated not very far from Gandhiji's Sabarmati Ashram, it stands in a dilapidated state, as a sad reminder of how little the freedom struggle offered the tribals and the nomadic communities of the country. The present Chharanagar is an ungainly slum of ill-planned houses just outside the old settlement. The total population of the Chharas in this ghetto today is nearly seven thousand.

The Chharas of Gujarat are called Sansis in Punjab and Kanjars in Rajasthan. They are not alone, there are nearly two hundred denotified communities in India and their total population may well be near sixty million. The infamy is mind-boggling. Can so many of our own people be stigmatised for such a long period? But the fate of the nomads in a society dominated by the value structure created by a sedentary culture has always been this: the nomad is always called a thief, whether he is one or not. The harm done to the gene pool because of a flawed history is incalculable. It is their hands, their skill and labour that made Indian culture aesthetically so rich. Today we are denying ourselves such a rich heritage.

IV

The Chharas were not the only denotified community that we encountered. For almost a whole year Mahasweta Devi, Laxman Gaikwad and I travelled hundreds of kilometres meeting Pardhis, Nats, Madaris, Vispadas, Turis, Chamthas, Gosavis, Wadars and many more such communities in small camps stationed along highways, precariously perched on village boundaries, hidden away in city slums, almost everywhere, but always trying to be invisible. We met them, tried to understand their situation, shared their agony and, wherever possible, tried to establish welfare works for them. But whatever else we did, we certainly fought each and every atrocity case. One day we would be standing in the Doki police station of Usmanabad district trying to register a criminal case of rape against the police inspector himself; and the next day we would be agitating for conducting a fresh post mortem for Pinya Hari Kale killed in police custody. Every fight brought together huge numbers of the invisible. Those who have been on the run for decades, halted for a while and looked up to us with some hope. In the process we kept discovering another India. For instance the India of the Bajanias, the drummer community of Gujarat.

On 3 November 1998, I read in the Gujarati daily *Sandesh* that a fifty-year-old man accused of stealing a green gourd was tied to a tree with a rope, beaten up and killed. I called the Commissioner of Police, Baroda and requested his assistance in reaching the family of the victim. At that point of time the police in Baroda was completely preoccupied with preventing communal tension. So I had to wait for three days to get the address I wanted.

On the afternoon of 6 November, Aruna Joshi and I went to see the widow of the man killed. Two policemen escorted us. The widow, Avliben, and her relatives were quiet. We too said very little to them and soon came back. I returned on my own the next morning to find out more about the incident, explaining that I had nothing to do with the police. They described the entire episode, step by step. They also showed me a two-page letter they had written to the Chief Minister of Gujarat, with a copy marked to the District Magistrate and the Police Commissioner. I got the letter photocopied. It said that Bhikabhai Bajania, who was employed as a watchman in a nearby factory, had prevented a Patel family from sending their cattle for grazing in the factory compound. That evening, the Patel family called Bikhabhai to their farm. After several hours he was brought back almost dead, and handed over to the Bajania community. He died within half an hour, but not before informing his wife and two sons that he had been tied to a tree with a rope and beaten up.

After his death the relatives reported the matter to the nearest police station, the Chhani station. A First Information Report was prepared; the police went to the farm and arrested three persons—the father and two sons—and brought them to the police station. A little while later, some influential persons in the area reached the police station. The Bajanias were told that the case should be reported to another police station since the incident had taken place outside the area of Chhani station. The two sons were released. The case moved to Bajwa police station. The father was taken into custody by the police there. Later on in the morning an MBBS doctor from the Bajwa Primary Health Centre conducted the post mortem examination of the body. The post mortem was carried out at the Sayaji General Hospital, but not recorded there. The letter added that the Bajania community apprehended further atrocity by the Patel community and asked for police protection. The letter had been sent by registered post. I met the members of the Bajania community several times to verify the details and to find out the reason for the murder. Was there something that the letter concealed? Was Bhikabhai involved in some crime? But all testimonies led to the conclusion that the story had no complications. It was simply the killing of a denotified tribal at the hands of a community that believes that all Bajanias are thieves because they are poor.

I made one or two unsuccessful attempts to meet the Police Commissioner. But when I persisted, he asked me to meet him in his office. In our meeting I told the Commissioner Kuldeep Sharma that it was surprising that only one person was arrested and charge-sheeted whereas all the reports mentioned three persons involved in the crime. He told me that he had not studied the case very carefully and would like to have some time to look into the file. I suggested that he should perhaps send one of his trusted officers to talk to the Bajanias. To my pleasant surprise he agreed to go there provided no one knew about his visit.

A week later, I drove Kuldeep Sharma to the Bajania locality. It was evening. The Commissioner had invited the chief of the detective branch of police to join us. The Bajanias did not know who my companions were. When we settled down, I asked them to narrate the episode at length. This time the story continued beyond the post mortem report. It went on to narrate how the sub-inspector of the Chhani police station had invited the Bajanias to negotiate with the Patels and not to press charges in exchange for an offer of seventy-five thousand rupees. They named the police officer, the place and date of his meeting them. Perhaps the Commissioner was convinced. But nothing happened for another ten days. I kept telephoning him. The Commissioner was occupied with other matters. I was becoming restless. When I indicated this to him, however, there was a call from the crime detection branch. Inspector Munshi came to my office and informed me that fresh investigations had started in the case. Within the next two days, he made a new charge sheet and arrested the other two persons suspected of involvement in the murder. The visits I made to the Bajanias created a bond of friendship and mutual trust between us. We were soon deeply involved in welfare work in the Bajania locality.

V

Attempts in isolated pockets, made at best in a piecemeal manner, will not bring about any significant change in the lives of the DNTs in India. For that to happen a radical change in popular perception must occur, and the state will have to squarely own the responsibility of the empowerment of these hounded communities. These changes are not likely to happen soon, or easily.

In May 1998 we had an official meeting with Smt Maneka

Gandhi in the Ministry of Social Justice. The Minister promised to set up welfare schemes for the DNTs. Project proposals were invited and submitted. In no time they were all lost in the jungle of files. Outside the Ministry, the DNTs continue to languish in despair. The only consolation they have received ever since the denotification was effected is perhaps from the National Human Rights Commission. Justice N. Venkatachaliah, its former chairperson, and Justice J. S. Verma, his successor, have both been sympathetic to this cause. During Justice Venkatachaliah's tenure as chairperson, the NHRC had set up a working group to prepare a report on the status of the DNTs. The Commission in March 2000 accepted the report. Chief Secretaries of eight states were invited to discuss the Report; and in consultation with them, the Commission passed the following resolutions:

1. To appoint a retired senior police officer of a high reputation in every state to watch the cases of atrocities against the DNTs.
2. To advise the National Police Academy and other institutions imparting training to police officers to reorient their syllabi.
3. To take the necessary steps leading to the repeal of the Habitual Offenders Act.
4. To direct Central/State Governments to make proper enumeration of the DNTs and to work out action plans in order to provide educational, employment and other infrastructure facilities to them.
5. To launch a massive information campaign aimed at bringing about change in the general attitude towards the DNTs.
6. To direct the National Sample Survey Organisation to make a special survey of the socio-economic conditions of the DNTs.

One hopes that India wakes up some day to the fact that the DNTs cannot go on endlessly suffering the colonial legal system, that they are becoming articulate and that the NHRC has already sounded a warning.

Thousands of DNTs assemble every year at Kaleshwari on the border of Madhya Pradesh and Gujarat for a mela. During the last mela, a hijra (hermaphrodites were included in the list of Criminal Tribes in the 1871 CT Act) said to me, 'Sir, I have heard it said that India is now a free country with her own laws. Is it true?' This is the question in the mind of every Indian nomad called thief.

VI

Dhamangaon was a station difficult to locate on a sixteen-hour journey from Baroda. I was told that the train would arrive there three hours after midnight. Fortunately, there was at least one more passenger in the Ahmedabad-Howrah Express that night heading for Dhamangaon. He helped me and Surekha not only to get down at the right station but also waited with us till the vehicle arranged for us showed up outside the station. From Dhamangaon to the Banjara *tanda* was a four-hour journey.

The moment we arrived there we found ourselves in the middle of a group of men singing and dancing. Atmaram Rathod, our host and an eminent writer in Marathi, was present to welcome us though he had been dancing and singing throughout the previous night. Besides, he had with him a documentation team from Siddharth Kak's Surabhi Foundation. They had been shooting till the early hours of the morning. After the welcome dance and song were over, we were taken to Atmaram's house. This was the place where his mother has spent all her life and where his brothers still continue to live.

The *tanda* or the settlement is on one side of a majestic hill and is surrounded by farms. The farms show signs of good care and steady irrigation. The houses number not more than sixty perhaps. Most of them are no more than dignified huts, but some have acquired brick and cement walls and at least two have polished tiles for the flooring. I had arrived in the middle of their holi celebration, and at least in those two days of my stay, the Banjaras looked a happy lot. Atmaram introduced me to a number of educated persons. His sister's husband runs a junior college; a cousin is employed in Bombay at the Public Distribution System as Inspector. There were others who had graduated or finished school. Girls too attend schools. The dance and song, the merriment, the well-tended farms and spread of education clearly show that the Banjaras are no different from other socially mobile classes of the Indian poor.

And yet in the evening, when they decided to play for my benefit the recording of a radio broadcast, suddenly things started acquiring a different colour. The recording narrated the ballad of their folk hero Senadas. Senadas started life in Karnataka as a cowherd and though the British tried to prevent him from migrating, he travelled upto the Sirohi district of Rajasthan. There he participated in an uprising against the British in order to fight the levying of tax on salt. One does not know if this is a sub-narrative of the Bhil uprising in the same area that took place for the same reason, in 1881, or whether the story of Senadas has found its way into the narrative of Govind Guru, another Banjara hero whose followers were massacred at Mangadh. The dates given by the Banjaras for the life span of Senadas are slightly earlier. After the uprising there seems to have been a period of obscurity in the hero's life. The last part of the narrative shows him in the form of a saint in Madhya Pradesh.

That Senadas still holds the Banjaras in thrall was very clear from the way they listened to the ballad with rapt attention. In fact the entire Banjara community feels bound to him the way the Sikhs feel bound to their gurus. Their language is called Gaud Banjara, perhaps a derivative of the Gaudi but more likely that of the Romani language mentioned by the tenth century theorist Rajasekhara. The history of the Banjaras between the tenth and the nineteenth centuries is lost in amnesia and some subconscious shape of a memory rises to the surface when they listen to the heroic tale of Senadas.

It does, again, when they share the meat of lambs killed ritually on the second day after holi. The lamb is bought with money collected from every household in the *tanda*. Its body is cut to pieces collectively and its head is roasted in full. The roasted ears are considered the most delicious, and children vie with one another for a bite of this. The ritual sacrifice connects the members of the community, the clan identity is reaffirmed through it. The Banjaras are spread over six clans, which are distributed over thousands of *tandas* between Rajasthan and Andhra through central India. They claim that their population is nearly twenty million, and though this count may seem exaggerated, there is no doubt that it *is* several millions considering that once every year they congregate in a *mela* of nearly one million near Yavatmal.

The way they organise themselves, find a place in the complex social order and shine in several newly acquired professions shows that the Banjars have an innate intelligence, which has helped them survive the Criminal Tribes Act. Their grace of manner and their natural wisdom show that theirs is a civilisation as old as any other in India. A Banjara doctor examined me in this *tanda* and diagnosed my problem of low blood pressure by taking my pulse. All that knowledge has gone now, of course. Maharashtra had a Banjara Chief Minister for many years and he did make efforts to resettle them. His efforts have paid off no doubt. Yet the popular imagery of Banjaras spawned through the Hindi cinema as snake-charming men and women of easy virtue continues to conceal the great revolution that has taken place among them. It is the same with the Chharas. People still refuse to acknowledge that given an opportunity the Chharas will excel in education and the professions.

On 4 March 2000, the Indira Gandhi Rastriya Manav Sangrahalaya and DNT-RAG organised an excellent mela of the DNT performers at Kaleshwari in Gujarat. We invited the Social Welfare Minister and the Secretary of Gujarat. They, however, did not attend the *mela*. The Social Welfare Minister also holds the portfolio for the Prohibition Department. When some of the Chharas were performing at Kaleshwari, the Prohibition Department organised an unprecedented raid on Chharanagar. The raid continued for several days, bringing in its wake, terror and arrests. The Chharas tried to meet the Minister but in vain. A few days later Mallika Sarabhai wrote a moving appeal to the citizens of Ahmedabad in the pages of *The Times of India*. Not only did the establishment look at this act with displeasure but in fact a section of the Gujarati press opened an attack on Mallika through their pages. The situation in Chharanagar itself was so tense and complicated that it was difficult to build any resistance movement there and Mallika had to face the press attack alone. She did it with exemplary courage and maturity. The desire for social transformation in the life of the Chharas, which has brought together a small group of young Chhara activists, still persists. They decided to organise an 'Evening of Goodwill' on 8 August 2000. During the evening they staged a new play *Tanuja Dipak Pawar*. Their earlier production *Budhan* had received wide acclaim. That the denotified communities are producing writers like Laxman Gaikwad, Atmaram Rathod and dramatic creations such as *Budhan* and *Tanuja* is a sure sign of the awakening and social change in these communities. The quickening of the imaginative life of a people precedes all major social changes. It is a sheer fortuitous coincidence that some of the great creative minds of our time such as Mahasweta Devi, Mallika Sarabhai, Bhupen Khakhar, P. Satchidanandan and Gayatri Spivak are actively engaged in the task of removing the stigma attached to the denotified communities. It is also very fortunate that the National Human Rights Commission has taken up the issue as one of national importance. Let us hope that the sordid saga of criminalisation of the innocent that began with the 1871 Criminal Tribes Act comes to an end in the twenty-first century. Nomads, too, are human beings.

3

Kikiyario
Adivasi Voice and Violence

I

An extremely sharp exclamation, abrupt, entirely unexpected, prolonged, defiant, jubilant, yet touched by pathos, an exclamation — part animal, part human and at its highest a somewhat divine sound, a sound such as only tribals know how to articulate; such a sound is called in Gujarati a *kikiyari.* In the tribal oral traditions it is never to be voiced in solo. It is to be used as a challenge to the companion in dance, as a collective approval in rituals, and as a war cry. This unscriptable cry is, therefore, always tribal and always in the plural, *kikiyario.* If tribals all over the world are a thousand times divided by clan, language, habitat and nomenclature, they are united by the *kikiyario,* the most public expression of the most elemental substratum of their being.

I have heard the *kikiyario* in many different parts of India, and every time they have reminded me of William Blake: 'Is that trembling cry a song ? Can it be a song of joy ?' Every time, I have felt that there are centuries of silence between the tribals and us and that they are offering the *kikiyario* as a bridge for us to cross that vast silence. Many times I have been transposed to that other world of ecstasy and pain like a character in a Mahasweta Devi novel, or as Verrier Elwin or Shankar Guha Niyogi had been in their time.

My destiny is intertwined with that of the tribal village, Tejgadh.

II

Tejgadh is situated on the border of Gujarat and Madhya Pradesh, ninety kilometres east of Baroda. The name of the village seems to have been drawn from the hill near by. The hill itself is now called Koraj Hill, but the relics of an eleventh century settlement seen at the foot of the hill show a fortified area which was possibly the Tejgadh fort at one time. There is, however, no memory of this fort in the local folklore. The only basis for hazarding this guess is that the Koraj Hill is linked to the chain of hills which ends with Pavagadh, a pilgrimage place near the seat of the medieval capital of Gujarat, Champaner.

The population of Tejgadh and the surrounding villages is predominantly tribal. These villages were ruled in the past by petty chieftains; and each one of them built for himself a fortification in the Rajput style. Tejgadh may have been one of those kingdoms. However, the present village is situated three kilometres away from the Koraj Hill. The oldest settler family there can recall a history not older than a hundred years. The family that claims to be the earliest family to settle in Tejgadh is of the merchant class. However, the largest segment of population is tribal; and their life-style is in continuity with the ancient and medieval tribal life-style in the region. Therefore there is not enough to assume that Tejgadh had been in existence for centuries prior to the settling of the merchant families there.

In terms of the village architecture, Tejgadh shows five layers of settlement. The earliest of these appears to have been the area of the village pond, near which a sixteen century step-well is still in existence, though it is out of use now. The pond is approximately four hundred metres away from the northern bank of the river Orsang. The next historical layer seems to be what is now known as Haridaspur, which is a cluster of about a hundred and seventy tribal families. But most of these families carry on the traditional animistic practice of worship and have preserved their sacred groves.

The third layer of habitation is at the foot of the Koraj Hill. However, the families settled there show no traces of lineage-relation with the historical Tejgadh fortification. They are all tribal families, and are clan relations of the families settled in Haridaspur. It is quite likely that they moved out of Haridaspur, subsequent to the decline of Tejgadh's political power, and claimed the land there for agricultural use. The fourth layer of settlement is the Limdi Falia, or the straw-market, around which the houses of the merchant class are built, and which are not older than a hundred years. The last layer of settlement is the Rohit Falia, or the colony of low caste Hindus, with houses built on the fringes of farms owned by the merchant class.

There are traces of three village ponds in Tejgadh. The oldest pond is closest to the river Orsang, and holds water even today. The second pond is close to the Rohitvas, about half a kilometre from the old pond; but it is now no more than a dry depression; a new road has been built to span it and it has been partially filled for that purpose. The third pond is near the Koraj Hill; it has completely dried up, but a view of the dry pond from the top of the hill shows how majestic it must have been at one time.

The river Orsang is a dry river with a sandy basin almost half a kilometre wide. It has water only during the monsoon months; but it turns to a trickle during the late-winter months, when the river bed is used for watermelon cultivation. There is no temple in the river bed or along the banks of the river. On the whole, the Orsang does not enjoy much centrality in the emotional life of the villagers in Tejgadh, nor does it enjoy a place of privilege in their festivals and rituals. It is rather seen as the line of natural defence.

There are no wells in Tejgadh which enjoy the status of community wells. Given that the tribals have their houses on their own farms, the existing wells are invariably agriculture-bound and are used by individual families. There are about sixty such wells, with a mouth of a diameter of twenty feet on an average, and a depth of eighty feet. The water supply for domestic use is arranged through pipelines. The village Panchayat manages the Tejgadh water works. A tube well is dug up for the purpose close to the Panchayat building. There are twelve hand pumps given to the village by the Taluka Development Office. They are spread over evenly in different parts of the village.

The Tejgadh village can be seen as a chain of rings, each larger than the previous one. Thus, the innermost ring forms the habitation of the Hindu merchants. The next, slightly larger, is the habitation of Muslims and the Harijans. The next is the habitation of tribals who consider themselves 'developed' tribals. The next ring, which is very large in scope is the habitation of the tribals. And the last ring, which covers an area of nearly twelve kilometres in length, has isolated habitation of the poorest of the tribals, who still survive on forest-gathering and farm labour. Of these, only the innermost ring, that is, the area where the Hindu merchant class resides, has a built drainage system. The gutters in Tejgadh are built with rubble-stone and are not covered. But most houses in the first two rings have latrines attached to the houses. The general practice is to build the latrine outside the main house, but within the compound area.

Three different places are used for cremation. One for the Hindu merchants and the Harijans, the second for the Muslims and the third for the tribals. All of them are at least a kilometre away from the village centre that is the Limdi Bazaar. For the disposal of the dead animals, there is only one place reserved, which is next to the railway track, since there are families that do the scavenging and the skinning of the dead animals. The disposal system is fairly efficient.

There are three public places of worship in Tejgadh. The most organised is the mosque, where prayers are offered punctually according to the customs of the Muslim families. There are two other temples, one of which has a Hindu deity of Mata or Laxmi and the tribal hero Bhathuji. There is one temple in Haridaspur which is devoted exclusively to Bhathuji. However, there is a public meeting hall for the Vaishnavas, within which idols of Krishna are displayed and worshipped on special occasions. Near the Koraj Hill, there is a beautiful temple precinct; but it is not in use now since the idols there are cracked. It shows relics of a Shiva temple and a broken Linga.

The Panchayat building is two-storied. Also, the Panchayat has built other buildings used for administrative work and for operating various government projects.

Tejgadh has a high-school, with an impressive and spacious building. It has three primary schools with fairly good structures, a primary health centre together with residential quarters for the medical staff and a veterinary doctor's service station.

Tejgadh is connected with telephone to the rest of the world, and has a regular supply of electricity through a two-phase feeder. Therefore, television, radio and microphones are used in Tejgadh. However, very few tribal families own television sets. The roads connecting Tejgadh with the taluka and district headquarters are of good quality and the main mode of transportation outside the village is the diesel-driven automobile. And on all sides it is surrounded by tribal villages.

III

When Gujarat was burning between 27 February and 4 March 2002, the tribal belt, on the eastern border of Gujarat was quiet. The only exceptions were the two districts of Panchmahals, for which Godhra is the main town. Elsewhere in the tribal areas, tribals, Hindus and Muslims continued to coexist peacefully. The only disturbing sight was the long lines of tribal labourers walking the distance from the curfew-bound cities to their villages, in some cases a walk of a hundred kilometres. They walked silently, carrying the burden of all their belongings on their heads, misery in their hearts, terrified like trapped animals.

Nearly sixty thousand tribal labourers migrate to Baroda every year in search of employment between October and March. From the third day of the riots these tribal labourers started returning to their village. No public transport was available to them. So, they decided to walk back like refugees trying to escape a devastated country.

The first Muslim shop to be set on fire in any tribal village was in Tejgadh. This case of arson took place on the evening of 4

March. During the night two more shops were torched. The rural branch of Baroda district police had not expected any reaction to the Godhra incident this late. On Tuesday, Senior DSP Keshav Kumar, who has prepared the first ever book on IPC in a tribal language for distribution among tribals, asked me to join him in his efforts to restore peace. When we arrived at Tejgadh, we saw a cloth shop being looted and set on fire by a mob. The DSP instantly fired tear gas shells and dispersed the mob. From there he proceeded to Chhota Udepur. He had expected five army trucks to arrive in the area for the night patrolling.

That night no army personnel were present in Tejgadh. More shops, more houses burnt in the village. Tejgadh has a miniscule Muslim population. Seventy-five per cent are tribals, fifteen per cent are Hindus and five per cent are Muslims. Those who burnt shops and houses came from the neighbouring villages, and in the initial stage were quite drunk. But once the first attack was over, the other villagers joined in on their own with no further need for instigation; the looting continued.

The incidents in Tejgadh displayed a method as well as a sequential growth in the theme of the disturbance. In the cities, at least for the first three days, the riots had a clear stamp of a well-researched and well-orchestrated strike. The attacks were marked with an amazing precision. As against this, the villages in Panchmahals, Kheda and Baroda districts displayed a blind anger. The incidents at Tejgadh were different from both. They showed that it was not included in the master plan of violence. Nor were the incidents unfolding in Tejgadh a frenzied reaction to the Godhra outrage.

The Muslim population in Tejgadh continued to stay in the village carrying out its daily work without any apprehension of intimidation. On that day Muslims in some other village were reportedly threatened by the local population; and it was initially maintained that all Muslims of Tejgadh went over to the other village to defend those Muslims. It is said that the residents of Tejgadh felt angered by this aggressive attitude of the Tejgadh Muslims. As a result one Muslim shop was set ablaze in Tejgadh on the evening of 4 March. It is said that Sarpanch Krishnakant Shah had tried to prevent those who wanted to start arson, but had to give up in the face of their pressure and threats. It is also said that the arsonists came from outside. After the incident, none in Tejgadh was prepared to name the arsonists. And nobody was able to say why all the Muslims had gone over to another village and why not even one of them returned to Tejgadh to save the shops, houses and vehicles that were burnt in regularly-tuned phases. No one was prepared to say how so much kerosene became available, and who led the mobs. And no one said why only properties belonging to Muslims were set on fire.

The Tejgadh carnage was leisurely; every day one or two shops were burnt. In the very first instance, the mob was collected from Timla, Koraj and Achhala segments of the Panchayat, all at a distance of one or two kilometres from Limdi Bazaar, the centre of the riots. In the second and third instances the distance increased. Tribals from neighbouring villagers wanted to have their share of the booty. The residents of Tejgadh had shut the doors of their houses and in a self-imposed curfew locked themselves in. When officially the curfew was imposed, it was only a matter of a technical detail.

The police force provided to watch the village was meagre, and after dispersing two or three rounds of mob attacks, it fell into the same kind of conspiracy of inaction that the villagers had already hatched. Thus, even on the twelfth day of the Tejgadh riots yet another house was burnt, with neither the villagers nor the police ready to intervene and avert the action. On the thirteenth and fourteenth days, one or two more houses were burnt down. The ritual continued. If the violence in the cities stood out by its precision and in other rural areas by its blind frenzy, the violence in Tejgadh stood out by its ritual quality. It showed a cold-bloodedness in slow-time. This ritual quality was a clear indication that at this end of Gujarat, the theme of communalism was taking a back seat and it had been taken over by the norms of tribal culture.

Therefore, when trouble began in Panvad, two days later and at a distance of thirty kilometres from Tejgadh, the stage for a tribal takeover of the riots was already set. Those who had interest in fanning the trouble had already started planting rumours that would provoke tribals. Among the rumours that I heard, the following five deserve mention.

1. A tribal dreamt that a majestic mahuda, the most sacred tree of the Rathwas, was chopped and used to block the road. Babadev, or the Babo Pithora God, was very angry and asked for revenge on those who had harmed the mahuda.
2. The police have come to believe that tribals have a mantra with which they can spellbind the police rifles; and therefore policemen are scared of using their weapons.
3. A certain Badwa, a shaman, has received the divine inspiration to become the biggest Badwa though his age is only twenty-two. He has learnt all aspects of magic and he cannot be killed. He will lead the tribals.
4. Muslims have been raping tribal women and kidnapping tribal girls and selling them in the cities.
5. Muslims have started taking away Kashmir (a place or a girl) by exploiting tribals, and they have kept fifty tribal women locked up.

The location of Panvad is unique. Almost twenty small and big villages can be reached from there in a very short time by walking cross-country. A number of Hindu sectarian movements have been active in the area for several years. Some Jain monks, probably from Rajasthan or Madhya Pradesh, have been living in a nearby village called Kawara and have a considerable influence on the people. The Muslim businessmen in Panwad are considerably affluent. Most of them are engaged in moneylending at an interest rate ranging between 60 to 120 per cent.

Whether it was because of the hatred for the moneylenders, or because of the rumours about the magical impediments to the police ability, the congregation of tribals at Panwad was alarmingly large. Newspaper reports say that their numbers were upto five thousand. But considering that every village sent about fifty to a hundred, the number of those who actually participated in the loot was a little less than two thousand at any given time.

The ritual quality introduced by the Tejgadh events was in evidence on a magnified scale in Panvad. This time the tribals were carrying their ceremonial bows and arrows with them. Normally, arrows are never used by them as weapons. When they want to kill someone, they use the sharp metallic *paliyu* or *dhariyu;* and when they want to fight a thief or an enemy, they try to use guns. Many of them possess a licence to keep guns, some buy them in illegal supply coming from Madhya Pradesh, which is just a few kilometres away. Arrows are used only by children for hunting birds. Very few birds are left in that area.

The first mob that attacked Panvad carried bows and arrows as a ritual decoration. But when it realised that mere mantras could not stop the policemen from firing, the next wave on the following day seems to have brought with it guns as well. Senior DSP Keshav Kumar, a courageous and conscientious officer, told me that he had to encounter tribals who stood before him and bared their chests daring him to fire. Such is their faith in the power of the rumoured mantra.

I was in Baroda when I learnt from HQ Officer Parmar that there was much trouble in Panvad, that one tribal had died in police firing and that the tribals had fired more than a hundred rounds. This was very disturbing news. The history of tribals in western India shows that once this kind of mood sets in, it takes a long time before things come back to normal.

I was also worried because in my view violence is not the way for tribal development. And the sole purpose of creating the Tribal Academy at Tejgadh was to teach tribals the ways of empowerment through constructive hard work.

I was in Tejgadh on 9 March, primarily to hand over a letter to the Administrator of Tribal Sub-plan in Chhota Udepur. This was the second Saturday of the month. This is normally a holiday, but some of the staff of the Tribal Sub-plan would be in the office to sort out the work that piles up as the financial year draws closer to its end in March. Saturday is the day of the weekly *haat* or market in Chhota Udepur. On this Saturday however there were no vendors in the *haat* and no buyers. In the last hundred years, the *haat* has remained closed not more than five times. Villagers from nearly seventy villages go to the Udepur *haat*. They all knew on 9 March that something unusual had been happening. The Panvad rumours spread rapidly through the medium of silence that the absent *haat* provided.

Sunday 10 March brought the news of further disturbance in the tribal areas. The trouble was spreading to other towns like Kawant and Chhota Udepur. Things were worse on 11 March.

Throughout the days of the riots, one could see trucks carrying petrol or kerosene making ritual trips to these towns. Obviously many mysterious elements had a part to play in the riots. But the forensic side of the riots was altogether neglected by the media, even *The Times of India* which carried an article on 14 March on the topic by Dipankar Gupta on its edit page. Similarly, the sociological aspect was largely overlooked. The Gujarati press, on the other hand, created an image of tribals as a gang of looters. But somewhere, despite the desire not to understand, not to analyse, the Gujarati press was closer to the truth of the matter. All of the newspapers in Gujarati described how the tribals were mounting attacks while letting out frightening *kikiyario*.

IV

The press kept asking me about the tribal situation and quoted me several times during the days of the riots. *Indian Express* reporter Swati Majumdar travelled with me to Tejgadh on 7 March to interview the residents there. However, she drew a blank as no one was prepared to risk making a statement. I continued to offer an analysis of the economic situation of tribals till 13 March. On that day District Magistrate Bhagyesh Jha and senior DSP Keshav Kumar were fired at by a tribal using a country gun. I thought I did not know enough about the situation and decided thereafter to keep quiet. It was on the same day that Jnanapith and Magsaysay award winner Mahasweta Devi wanted me to send a report for the Calcutta based *Aaj Kaal*. I wrote the following:

> Riots spread to Panvad four days later and to Kawant seven days after they had erupted in Tejgadh. In Panvad the police had to resort to firing hundred and ten rounds on a single day; and the tribals who had been emboldened by then fired on police in return. The riots are still continuing and when they are brought under control in one village, another village goes up in flames.
>
> Everybody has been asking why tribals, who do not have any sympathy with Hindu fundamentalism, have got involved in the riots ?
>
> In this area, the literacy among women is less than 20 per cent, the rate of interest for loans from money lenders ranges between 60 to 120 per cent. Nearly 30 per cent population is carrier of sickle cell anaemia and three per cent of them confirmed sicklers. Medical facilities are inadequate and for the last three years the area has gone through a severe drought. Obviously the Gujarat tribals' concern for economic development is far greater than for the construction of a temple. Whoever initiated the riots by distributing liquor and supplying petrol and guns does not know that a short term political gain for a party will create a long term problem of tribal insurgency.
>
> I have been working in Tejgadh and the surrounding villages. Mahasweta Devi has helped us to establish a tribal academy there. Mahasweta Devi and I would like all Indians to know that the tribals of Gujarat are unnecessarily being dragged into the Mandir politics. What they need and want is a decent education, health and employment and not temples and religious leaders. Bread, and not god, is what they want.

Throughout the day on 19 March, I had heard that it was almost certain that Chhota Udepur which had remained tense but free from violence would go the same way as Kawant, Panvad and Bodeli.

By that evening some arrests had been made; and it appeared that the ring-leaders had been arrested. The fifteen-day tribal riots in Chhota Udepur taluka were over. No house or shop was burnt on 19 March in Tejgadh, Panvad, Bodeli. By the morning of 20 March the tone had changed. There was panic among the tribals. Their concern now was how not to get arrested.

However, the peace that appeared certain on 20 March, turned out to be a mirage when three days later three more structures were set on fire in Tejgadh. Bodeli too remained smouldering; and, of all places, Chhota Udepur which had remained calm during the previous three weeks started looking tense. Curfew had to be imposed there in the fourth week since the riots began. The fire lit in the tribal region was showing no signs of dying.

From the perspective of the tribals it is necessary to raise some questions about the riots : Did the tribal population of Chhota Udepur region have any plans of rising up in a revolt ? Was there any explicit or latent movement in the area bordering on a militant opposition to the state ? Had the communal BJP made such inroads in the tribal life that the spirit of Hindutva overtook the local tribal culture ? In other words, how much of the Muslim persecution in the tribal regions of Gujarat during the riots of March 2002 was *tribal* in character, and how much of it was a measure of the BJP's success ? Answers to these questions are important to understand the riots as well as the tribal situation.

One aspect of the entire episode that stood out from the very beginning of the riots was that the persecution of Muslims in Tejgadh and Panvad had not been spontaneous, even as planned by the Sangh Parivar elsewhere in Gujarat. Tejgadh took five days to react and Panvad nearly nine days. Besides, the awareness about Kashmir, Ayodhya and cross-border terrorism has been almost negligible in the tribal villages. Many villages in the region have sarpanchs who are illiterate or semiliterate; and the electronic media is almost absent in these villages.

During those days one educated young Rathwa friend sent a

note to me. It contained his reflections on the demise of a tree. This was the giant neem, called Limda in Gujarati and which gave the name 'Limdi Bazaar' to the area in which arson was going on. The neem was set on fire by the arsonists. It had been standing there for more than a century; and it was burnt alive. It burnt for ten days. Slowly, ritually. The note sent to me by Arjun Rathwa said:

> Did the Limda have any religion apart from giving shade to the wayfarers ? Was it not like an adivasi, neither Hindu nor Muslim ? Why have they destroyed it ? Was it anybody's enemy ? Adivasis too are being destroyed like the neem. They are neither Hindus nor Muslims. But now they are being uprooted altogether.

I would like to consider this note as typical of the tribal non-involvement in communal politics. What was then the source of the wrath let loose on the Muslim community ? The most viable answer to this question is that the tribals were made to fight a proxy war on behalf of the baniyas.

V

Two incidents of the earliest days of the Gujarat riot will illustrate tribal unwillingness to participate in the communal frenzy. On the evening of 27 February, a truck carrying Muslim passengers from Panchmahals sped through Tejgadh, causing another vehicle, a jeep carrying passengers, to pull closer to the edge of the road. Such jeeps, the most popular mode of transport in the area, are impossibly over-crowded, and passengers, hang on to the vehicle on all sides. This one pulled itself so close to the edge of the road that four passengers, three men and a woman, died on the spot, crushed between the vehicle and the trees on the side of the road. The villagers knew that the other vehicle, which had caused the accident, was carrying Muslims, not from any other district but from Panchmahals, not on any other day but the day of the Godhra outrage. The villagers in Tejgadh allowed the vehicle safe passage without any expression of anger, which under the circumstances would have been justified even on an ordinary day.

The second incident happened on 28 February in Haridaspur, the oldest segment of Tejgadh. Haridaspur, which has 170 households, all having a clan relationship. The people of the Haridaspur had gathered during the forenoon to cremate and mourn the death of an inhabitant. In that assembly of approximately 1,200 people, some of the elected members of the Panchayat from another locality had been talking of avenging the Godhra incident. But they did not find favour for their inflammatory appeals even after the gathering had been served the ritual drink of wine. This was the support, or lack of it, to the Hindutva appeal on the day on which all newspapers had headlines about the Godhra carnage. Persons present during the cremation have reported to me (on conditions of anonymity) that an announcement was made that free supply of kerosene and liquor would be made to those who had the 'courage' to attack Muslims.

The Sarpanch of Tejgadh was approached by the trouble-makers on 1 March and asked for his participation in burning Muslim families; he is reported to have refused to allow any violence within the limits of his Panchayat. It appears that on 2 and 3 March, the communal section of the village changed its argument by giving up the purely communal angle and bringing in the more acceptable business angle. It said that the Muslim businessmen had become too arrogant and, to use the equivalent of the local idiom, that 'they have put on too much fat.' This argument clinched the issue; and on the evening of 4 March, when in Chief Minister Modi's ridiculous phrase, 'the riots had been brought under control within a record seventy-two hours', the first Muslim shop was set on fire.

This shop was owned by the fifty-five year old Yakub Khatri and had wares like biscuits and mints. Yakub Khatri owned five acres of agricultural land and his brother Ghanibhai was a respected figure in the affairs of the Tejgadh mosque. However, the sweetmeat shop does not give a clear picture of Yakub's financial status. He owned a large house and two more shops, selling foodgrains, cutlery, bangles and shoes, at a distance of eight hundred metres. Obviously, by targeting Yakub Khatri it was possible for the Hindu communal force to combine the theme of religious revenge with that of business competition.

During this instance of arson, the Muslim community in Tejgadh was still present in the village. It tried to counter the attack, but the mob gathered was large, and its resistance could not have been adequate. There were no policemen present at the scene of this crime. Quite obviously, during the three preceding days, the Muslims in Tejgadh had feared such an attack and had already prepared themselves to flee. The riots that began during the late hours of the afternoon continued during the evening with two more shops gutted by fire. During the night, all Muslims fled. No one seemed to know where they had sought asylum. It was rumoured that during the Yakub Khatri episode, Muslims had fired shots at the mob, implying that they were in possession of unlawful weapons and strengthening the stereotype of all mosques being places for hoarding weapons.

The next shop destroyed was owned by Kadarbhai, aged fifty-five, and owner of a flour mill, a cloth shop and a grocery shop. Dilawarbhai, forty, who owned a cloth shop and an adjacent shop of cutlery and shoes, was the next in the line of fire. Ahmedbhai, fifty-five, owned a foodgrains business and also hired out materials like pandals and public address systems for public functions. Nasirbhai, who too had a cutlery and foodgrains business followed in the line. At this juncture, the communal interest seems to have faded from the minds of the rioters. Those who organised the riots and funded them appear to have started looking at this operation purely as a business activity of eliminating the competition and creating a total control over the market; and those who participated in the riots appear to have started looking at the incidents as an opportunity to loot in the manner of an unusual public ritual. I have already commented on the ritual aspect of the Tejgadh riots and how it was appropriated by the Panvad riots which were just about breaking out at this juncture.

It was at this juncture too that the five rumours listed previously were planted because an internal contradiction had started breaking up the momentum, which the communal force had managed to create with great difficulty. The contradiction appears to have come up from the intention of the tribals to attack businessmen (who invariably have been moneylenders), and the baniya intention of causing an attack on Muslim businessmen alone. The Hindu baniyas who were behind the riots started fearing that the tribal enthusiasm for looting shops would lead to their own shops becoming targets. Therefore, once again the riot machine at Tejgadh chose to burn down the two shops of Yakub Khatri, which were spared during the first round of arson. It appears that owing to Yakub's familial tie with Gani, an attack on him looked like an attack on the Tejgadh mosque.

The next to be attacked was an elderly and respectable Muslim popularly known as Lakhpati (meaning millionaire) and who had been a kingpin in the local moneylending business, though in recent years his fortunes had been sinking. When communal passions were ignited, the rioters had no time to think of the financial status of their victims. Therefore, the house of Bhikha the tailor, Fakirbhai the poor peasant with a landholding of less than an acre, the house of Yusufbhai Khatri, a retired prison-clerk, were reduced to ashes. But, the business interest in the riots did not wane at all; and therefore a warehouse where Muslim merchants used to stock their wares was also set on fire. The houses which the Muslim inhabitants had deserted were searched by the mobs and vandalised. The last one to be attacked was Basheer Khatri's shop selling soft drinks and cloth. The police presence in Tejgadh throughout the days of the riots, a long period of two weeks, was more marked by its complicity than by its inadequacy. What is the most explicit comment on the motive and the nature of the riots is that not even once after 4 March did the Panchayat members or the local Hindu baniyas make an attempt to dissuade the rioters.

Their only act of 'grace' was to spare the house of Shabirbhai, who has been an elected member of the Panchayat and represents, at present, the Muslim community in Tejgadh. Thus the five hundred odd Muslim inhabitants of Tejgadh were 'punished' for someone else's attack on the S6 coach of the Sabarmati Express at Godhra, and, more importantly, for competing with the Hindu moneylenders in the tribal area. Similarly throughout the few days of the intense rioting in Panvad, one repeatedly heard that the riots were meant to teach a lesson of their lives to the Muslim moneylenders who had 'put on too much fat'.

VI

It would be completely wrong to assume that the rioting in these tribal villages was, at any stage, in support of Hindutva. The facts show that this is far from the truth. There had to be a considerable amount of coaxing before any tribal village joined in the riots. There was a free use of intimidation too. Generally, a group of fifteen to twenty persons went to the sarpanch of a village to ask him to give forces for attacking Muslims. Generally, one or two of the ringleaders spoke. They promised protection from the law to all those who joined and threatened those who refused the 'invitation'. Since the instigators belonged to the ruling party, it was very intimidating to encounter such promises and threats. Before and during the main days of the Panvad riots, a young Rathwa - who became the Shaman in the widespread rumour - used to promise Rs. 2,00,000 to the family of any possible casualty. Alternatively he would threaten with dire consequences those who refused. Actually, the Rathwa had neither the wealth to make the promised compensation, nor the political clout to actualise the threats. It must also be kept in mind that Rathwas are a people of very few words, do not speak beyond a monosyllable in their normal conversation, and very rarely tell lies. If a Rathwa commits a murder, it is often said by the police, he will report to the police station himself and confess to his crime. Therefore, when this person was going round making the offer, he was in all probability not using empty words. Surely, other persons with so much moneys to offer had backed him; and clearly, he was working at their behest. All in all, therefore, the tribal riots were organised by the moneylenders, even if the legal evidence to establish this fact will be slow in coming. The combing operation taken up by the state following the riots will be a superficial exercise and will end when a large number of poor rioters are booked under the law on the basis of stolen goods such as utensils, foodgrains and cloth found in their dwellings.

There have been excellent studies on the role of the *sahukar* in the Panchmahals during the nineteenth century and on how the *sahukars* generated the tribal resistance movement in order to protect their own right to trade salt in Sirohi district of Rajasthan. Thanks to these studies, one can say with certainty that the tribals in western India have remained under the yoke of the moneylender for centuries.

Particularly from the time the tribals lost their sovereign rights over the forests and had to identify themselves with a given piece of land which was recorded in the books of the Revenue Department, the ability of tribals to meet any contingencies requiring large cash payments has gone down considerably. The land available for cultivation gets divided with every passing generation, though such divisions are not necessarily reflected in the land records. In rain-fed agriculture, the tribal tiller manages to produce just enough for subsistence; and even a single year of poor rains leads to endless indebtedness. Bank operations in tribal areas have been shamefully anti-tribal. In the first place, the service branches are not easily accessible in terms of their geographical location. Even when they exist, their operations have no place or thought for the tribals despite directives from the zonal offices and agencies like NABARD. It is a fortunate tribal with whom a bank manager has entered into any conversation. Rarely is there a tribal who does not get insulted when he enters a bank. Then, the documentation part of any bank deal is beyond a tribal to cope with. As against this, the private moneylender asks for no documents. He knows by name every tribal who comes to him as a client. His terms are sufficiently flexible to accommodate modifications in the schedule of payment should it be required due to failure of the monsoon. In exchange for all this kindness the moneylender charges a high rate of interest.

It ranges from five to twelve rupees per month, that is, 60 to 144 per cent for a year. The interest for the first three months is deducted from the principal at the time of the lending, which means that an amount of seventy is handed over to the borrower out of a notional hundred rupees if the interest is 120 per cent. The loan is not required to be repaid in cash. The moneylender accepts foodgrains, forest produce or timber in lieu of cash at a rate that he will decide according to the going rate in the local market. If the foodgrains are not enough to repay the loan with the interest, the borrower approaches another moneylender in order to procure cash to repay the first loan in full. Two centuries of this lending practice have made the moneylenders prosperous beyond imagination, and the tribals indebted beyond redemption.

The moneylenders reside in the larger villages like Tejgadh or Panvad or in towns where the weekly *haat* is held. The tribal peasants go to the *haat* every week and make it a point to wish the moneylenders. This, they think, adds to their creditworthiness. This also helps in doing economic policing for the moneylenders.

The politicians too are greatly dependent on the moneylenders for their political success, for the *sahukars* control the vote banks for them. It is almost impossible for the politicians not to be sensitive to the views and interests of the moneylenders. Even when the elected representatives of people belong to tribes in the areas of reserved constituencies, they are severely restricted from undertaking developmental activities that will harm the interests of the moneylenders. Therefore, while one finds that an impressive developmental activity of a cosmetic nature takes place in tribal areas, economic empowerment is deliberately given a back seat. Poor infrastructure, chronic cash-crunch, pervasive unemployment, illiteracy, and technological backwardness, which in other sectors are considered unfavourable for economic growth, are the necessary and minimum conditions for the growth in the private moneylending sector. The situation may differ in degree from one tribal district to another, but the general pathology of tribal underdevelopment and chronic indebtedness does not.

VII

About a decade back, when I began my study of tribal languages and culture, I was not aware of the power of the moneylender in tribal society. Former Governor of the Reserve Bank and Director of London School of Economics, Dr I.G.Patel had remarked to me in 1996: 'Once you start making an economic intervention in tribal life, you will come up with massive opposition.' Therefore, when a Trustee of Bhasha Research Centre Dr. Ravikant Joshi suggested that we introduce a micro-credit scheme for tribals in Tejgadh, I wanted to look for a non-radical cover for taking anything so radical to the tribals. We found that the Rotary Club in Baroda was ready to collaborate. But soon the Rotarians were tired of operational difficulties; and we found, on the other hand, that the tribals enthusiastically joined the scheme. The next requirement was to create a channel for the sale of their agricultural produce without the agency of the middle-man. So, we brought in Trifed, a corporation established by the Union Government specifically for this purpose. This was too much of a threat for the grain merchants and the moneylenders. I remember how angry they were with me and how they threatened a hunger strike if I did not instantly abandon the Trifed operation. But even at that time I was not aware of the real cause of the anger which became clear as the micro-credit scheme progressed and expanded. Gradually, I started hearing that both the Congress and the BJP were against our activity, and politicians from both sides started making angry representations against our activity in the high offices in Gandhinagar. At least two successive District Magistrates of Vadodara have told me to focus only on language research and not to do extension work involving activities like micro-credit. 'There is a strong opposition to your work and it will increase in future,' they said. Having experienced the intensity of the anger of the moneylenders, I am not surprised that it has been the most focal cause for the brutal attack on the Muslim moneylenders. This could have been averted had the spirit of the Constitution been taken into consideration by those in whom the Constitution vests certain special powers for the welfare of the weaker sections. By March 2000, I had become fully convinced that the problem of tribal indebtedness would result in a major upheaval if it was not tackled well in time. Therefore I wrote to the Governor of Gujarat Sundersinh Bhandari drawing his attention to the problem and urging him to use his special powers under Article 5 (2,6) of the Fifth Schedule:

> During my work with tribal communities of Gujarat I have repeatedly come across the frightening phenomenon of long-term indebtedness. I have noticed that tribals have been borrowing sums from private moneylenders residing in taluka towns and commercial centres at an exorbitant rate of 80 per cent to 100 per cent interest in order to meet their needs of cash required at the beginning of the agricultural season or during weddings and festivals. They are invariably not able to pay back the interest let alone the original sum borrowed. Recently we formed 100 Self Help Groups under our Micro-Credit programme with a membership of about 1200 families. Our experience showed that without an exception, the families have been victims of the exploitative money lending system. On the basis of this survey and my earlier work in other tribal areas of Gujarat, I have come to the firm conclusion that no economic development of the tribals will be even remotely possible if nearly 4.5 million of the 7 million tribals in Gujarat are groaning under the burden of indebtedness.
>
> On behalf of these 4.5 million tribals of Gujarat somehow managing to survive and trying to be free from the acute indebtedness, I most sincerely appeal to you to use the powers vested in Governor's office under the provisions of the 5th Schedule, Part B, 5 (2,6) which states :
>
> 'The Governor may make regulations for the peace and good government of any area in a State which is for the time being a Scheduled Area.
>
> .....such regulations may -
>
> (c) regulate the carrying on of business as moneylender

> by persons who lend money to members of the Scheduled Tribes in such area.'
>
> I would further like to pray that all Scheduled Areas (inclusive of the 9 tribal sub-plan areas) be covered by the regulation.
>
> The regulation should prevent from the date of the issuance of regulation lending of short term or long term loans, involving small or large sums, in cash or kind, by charging interest which is higher than the current bank rates of interest.
>
> It should also declare all debts received by any tribal person null and void and not binding on the borrower in case such debts were received prior to the date of the issuance of the regulation.
>
> The regulation should make lending of money or kind at the rate of interest which is higher than the prevailing bank rate of interest to tribal persons, a non-bailable criminal offence.
>
> It is also necessary to place a general moratorium on all and every deed of land transfer for one full year from the date on which the regulation comes into effect.
>
> I hope that Your Excellency will take a serious view of the exploitative practice and decide on the matter expeditiously. I have no doubt in my mind that in consonance with the spirit of the Constitution and in the interest of social justice, our State needs to bring a permanent end to a great social evil which has made tribal life a curse.

Subsequently, I, Mahasweta Devi and Bhupen Khakhar met him to discuss the problem. He argued that there was not enough factual data to support our claim. Our argument was that moneylenders on their own would not submit their books of accounts to the government. The decision would have to be made on the basis of his discretion and judgment. He assured us that our petition would be sent to the Minister in Charge of Tribal Development. Then Mahasweta Devi sent a similar request to the President of India. No reply to our letters has ever been received.

VIII

The use of bows, arrows and guns by the tribals against the police during the riots is not sufficiently explained by an analysis of their indebtedness to the moneylenders and being coaxed by them into eliminating the Muslim competitors. The mob-militancy of the Rathwa tribals has other sources. In order to explain those we need to look at the sociology of Panvad more closely and also how its confrontation with modernity has produced unique discontents.

Among the tribal towns of Vadodara district, Panvad is closest to Madhya Pradesh. The Bhils, who are no different from the Rathwas in language or customs and who live on the other side of the completely notional border, were at one time notified during the British rule under the Criminal Tribes Act (1871). The reason for that notification was that earlier they had worked as seasonal soldiers for the Maratha princes in Indore and Dhar. But their 'denotification' in 1952 has left them no real choice either, a life of occasional crime being their only option. As a result of the possible menace of the denotified Bhils across the border, the villages surrounding Panvad have launched a massive deforestation of the low hills, in order to increase the range of visibility as a measure of security. Deforestation of this region was encouraged by the timber merchants at Chhota Udepur who controlled the Forest Kamdar Sangh during the 1960s.

All ecological dangers that follow deforestation have been visited upon the Panvad region. Agricultural income in that area is lower in comparison with a corresponding agricultural holding in other tribal areas of the district. As a way out of this, Panvad tribals have moved to literacy and education more hopefully; but for want of an institution of higher learning in the near vicinity, the young tribals end up with high school education and little or no employment. Many migrate to places like Surat to work as diamond cutters and to Kutch, to work as construction or agricultural labour. For many years the Gujarat Mineral Development Corporation's fluorspar project at nearby Kadipani used to provide employment. But some years back it ran into rough weather due to legal and administrative hassles. Since then the young tribals in the area have taken to drug-trafficking and a small amount of arms-selling. The arms are brought in from Madhya Pradesh, taken to Vadodara and then the customers are located in the region and directed to Vadodara for a bargain purchase. Those who make this easy money then move on to becoming small time moneylenders and start acquiring Hindu names and traits. They are the ones who become hospitable to various sect movements. These new arrivals in the Hindu fold have been the special constituency of the Hindutva movement in the area.

When we started the micro-credit scheme in 1999, we also formed self-help groups (SHGs) of tribals in the villages surrounding Panvad. The groups were Kanalwa (2), Chimli (1), Dungargam (2), Shihada (17), Jhanjharjhol (7), Panvad (9), Modhalia (4), Rangpur (1), Jhakha (1), Kavra (14), Ganthiya (4), Gabadiya (4). During the three years of drought, while the SHGs in other villages had great difficulty in repaying the small bank loans, these SHGs would suddenly come up with wads of bank notes and repay loans of several groups on a single day. I was surprised to find on many occasions that the notes brought for repayment were serially numbered. Obviously they did not reflect collections from the poor tribals, which in the case of the SHGs in other villages used to come in the form of soiled and old currency notes such as labourers keep with them. Obviously, the moneys came from a bank withdrawal. The members of the SHGs had, in principle, no other bank accounts than the ones we were helping them to operate. It is only in retrospect that I can say that the amounts came from moneylenders, from a loan given to a group leader for bringing the micro-credit scheme to a halt. The Panvad tribals were quite prepared to go back to 120 per cent interest rate from the bank's mere twelve per cent. For the young, neo-Hindu, semi-educated, unemployed, indiscriminate generation, the Hindu moneylender has become the role-model, and drugs and unlicensed arms the new sources of a sense of power.

The ultimate source of violence is the mind and not the weapons in one's possession. The tribal mindset is not feudal, but it is certainly medieval. It is not feudal because of the tribal attitude to state formation in which the clan replaces the state. But precisely for the reason of preserving clan autonomy and clan purity, the attitude to women among the tribals is dictated by a limitless fear of women's pollution by an external agency. When in a rare case a tribal woman expresses the desire to marry a person outside the particular tribal clan, invariably there is bloodshed. While girls have the freedom to choose their life partners within the clan and without the slightest opposition from the family or relatives, they have no freedom to extend the choice beyond the male members of the clan. This social code, however, is coming increasingly under stress from the rapidly changing economic context.

The tribal district north of the Panvad - Chhota Udepur area, that is the Panchmahals, has witnessed social transition of women's status on an unprecedented scale. Among the tribals, dowry is given by the groom to the bride's parents. The bride-price among most tribes is nominal or notional. But, among the heavily indebted Panchmahals tribals, this bride-price has come to be perceived as an alternate source of income. In recent years it has soared to 60,000 rupees, while earlier it used to be one or two thousand. The result is that as soon as the wedding takes place, the groom takes the bride with him to a city like Ahmedabad or Vadodara and the two start working as labourers so that the huge amount borrowed from relatives and moneylenders can be repaid over a period of several years.

The condition of the migrant women labourers in the cities is pitiable. They have to face, among other things, sexual exploitation from the labour contractors and the city-dwellers. Now the tribals in Panchmahals have started receiving lucrative offers from caste Hindus for purchase of their daughters. The tribals in Panvad area are familiar with these changes. To the east of Panvad is Madhya Pradesh. The tribal women here have faced humiliation worse than those in the Panchmahals. Some of the denotified tribal communities such as the Bedias and Kanjars in that area have come to a situation where forcing young girls into sex work is seen as most natural.

In the Panvad region the fear of violation of tribal women has gripped the tribal psyche. The police records for the period 1990 to 2000 show that the highest number of murders in the region are related to the perceived fear of a woman being taken away. Therefore, it would have been surprising if the tribals in that region had not reacted violently after being given a generous diet of rumours about fifty of their women being sexually abused by Muslims. This rumour was not used in Tejgadh by those who planned the pogrom, and therefore the scale of violence in Panvad was higher than in Tejgadh.

There is one more reason for tribal militancy in the area, but the scientific validity of that reason is not yet generally acceptable to sociologists. This reason originates in a biological condition resulting from a disease generally known as the sickle cell anaemia. I myself became aware of the possible connection between the proclivity to violence and the genetic cell disorder when, as a Jawaharlal Nehru Fellow, I had been working on a study of violence in India during the early nineties. At that time the case of malnutrition of the Korku tribals in Amaravati district of Maharashtra had been receiving considerable media attention. About the same time, the Chandrapur tribal area in Maharashtra had started showing a pronounced militant tendency. I kept following the matter patiently for some years, and then decided to convene a conference of doctors, anthropologists and researchers working on the sickle cell problem. Doctors from many states, including Dr. Kenneth Bridges of the Harvard School of Medicine, were present.

Since I am opposed to violence as a means of social change, and since I was aware of the alarming scale of the incidence of Sickle Cell anaemia in Chhota Udepur region, I approached District Magistrate Anil Mukim and presented the note to him in September 2000.

Anil Mukim thanked me for drawing his attention to the problem and told me that he had forwarded the note to the Health Secretary in Gandhinagar. On my part, I initiated several check up camps with the help of Dr. R.Z. Patel of Baroda Medical College for detection of sickle cell patients and started offering relief supply of folic acid tablets to the detected patients.

IX

Those who want to understand the unexpected rise of violence among the tribals of Gujarat may find it useful to note that during a short period of six weeks preceding the March 2002 riots, in a small segment of Tejgadh, namely Haridaspur, with a population of 1200, the following sudden deaths had occurred :

1. Mansukhbhai Dalasukhbhai, age 55
2. Chikhabhai Dalasukhbhai, age 45
3. Kanchanbhai Chhaganbhai, age 40
4. Kamriben Tersinghbhai, age 40
5. Maniabhai Ruplabhai, age 40
6. Singliben Nathiyabhai, age 55
7. Sansubhai Soriyabhai, age 13

In addition, two children of age 10 and age 1 respectively, died, whose names are not on my record. Not all of them died of sickle cell. In fact, the general life span for sickle cell patients ranges between 10 to 25. Many of these, therefore, have to be described as deaths due to malnutrition and medical inattention. No government likes to accept the fact that many poor persons die for want of sufficient diet.

On 15 August 2001 there had been eight cases of starvation in Chhattisgarh, which made those tribals eat a dead bullock's meat leading to their death. At that time I wrote to Prime Minister Atal Behari Vajpayee:

> On the Independence Day, as we were watching you

speak to the nation, we also received the shocking news of the death of ten tribals in Chhattisgarh because of food poisoning caused after they ate the meat of dead bullocks. That tribals are driven to eating dead animals out of hunger which has no other means to assuage it is a shame for all of us who can get two square meals a day.

This situation could have easily been averted, had the funds available for tribal development been put to use. Some days back I read a report in Gujarat *Samachar* that the Gujarat State has not used even one rupee from the grants available for tribal development during this financial year. A similar situation in Bengal is already being investigated by order of the Calcutta High Court after Smt. Mahasweta Devi filed a case. The Tribal Development Ministry of Central Government has mooted a foodgrains bank scheme; but I understand that its implementation in Orissa has been half-hearted and the scheme has more or less failed there. If your Government were to bring all the tribal villages under the foodgrains bank scheme in the States with tribal population, leaving out the Northeastern states, the total investments required would not exceed Rs. 800 crores (at Rs. 65,000 per bank as per the scheme). I, therefore, do not understand why your Government cannot provide food security to the tribals of India. The Korkus of Maharashtra have been dying of malnutrition; the tribal women in Rajasthan and Gujarat are being regularly sold for feeding their hungry families; the sickle cell anaemia which is already affecting nearly three per cent of tribal population, is further aggravated by want of adequate food. In Gujarat alone, where we have carried out testing, an estimated two lakh persons are awaiting slow but certain death due to the SCA. The situation of denotified tribals is even worse, because added to

> hunger they have to face persecution. If, under these circumstances, the Government remains passive, food security cannot be provided, what is the use of Independence for us ?
>
> On my part, I have taken a vow to skip one meal a day throughout my life and to mobilise tribals in village to fight the oppressive situation till such a time as there is not even one hunger death among the tribals. I request you on behalf of the tribals of India to kindly do something concrete in this regard.

Subsequently, I met the Prime Minister on 13 September at his residence in Delhi, and emphasised the need to establish foodgrain banks in all tribal villages. Mahasweta Devi, Laxman Gaikwad, Haribhau Gaikwad and Ajay Dandekar were present at the meeting which lasted twenty-five minutes. I have learnt through newspapers that the Central Government did declare the scheme of foodgrain banks for 1,16,000 villages. However, such foodgrain banks had not been established in Chhota Udepur prior to my pleading with the Union Tribal Secretary S. K. Naik and Commissioner for Tribal Development Ramji Rai. The result of that campaign is that forty villages of Chhota Udepur will get FGBS from April 2002.

But, if a large section of population is left to fend for itself to face poverty, hunger, exploitation, and if their semi-literacy and unemployment lead them to a harsh zone of conflict of social values, if the new role models are based on the idea of making easy money, it is more likely than not that the space for irrational militant tendency will be created. Panvad could not have been an exception.

Yet, it would be wide of the mark to believe that the tribals in Chhota Udepur and Kawant talukas of Vadodara district had at any time prior to the riots of March 2002 made any plans or conspiracy of an armed attack on the *haats* in Tejgadh or Panvad, or that there was any leadership locally available with a political ideology in which violence is the means of social change.

On 13 March, the District Magistrate Bhagyesh Jha and Senior DSP Keshav Kumar were shot at with a country rifle while they were in the field; and on 20 March, correspondent Sajid Shaikh filed the following report, which appeared on page 1 of the *Times of India.*

> *Tribals Fox Cops with Guerrilla Warfare Tactics*
>
> The clock seems to have turned back to the medieval times in this district. At least that's what the tribals' warfare tactics during the riots revealed.
>
> Numbers were counted as strength, bows and arrows were the chief weapons and adjoining hills and ravines were regarded strategic locations to mount attacks on the 'enemy'.
>
> The deft usage of their traditional weapons and surprise attacks foxed both the police and the public. After a week of skirmishes with the tribals, fifty-nine policemen were injured, two people killed, several houses charred, vehicles torched and shops looted.
>
> Their modus operandi : Hordes of tribals would appear from the woods, make strange noises, rain arrows, pelt stones and vanish in thin air after inflicting damage. Even the convoy of District Collector Bhagyesh Jha and Senior Superintendent of Police Keshav Kumar was not spared.
>
> 'They appeared from nowhere and started shooting arrows. Later, gunshots were heard and we told our men to take position. They made noises as if communicating among themselves and when we upped the defences they vanished as fast as they had appeared,' Jha said.
>
> 'The scene was like a chapter straight out of a history book. We chased one of the miscreants deep into the woods till he gave out a tribal cry and his accomplices appeared on the fringes. They took position and started shooting arrows at us,' Kumar recalled.
>
> While the collector and SSP were given a sneak peak of the medieval warfare tactics, the full length feature of their strategy was evident in Kawant, Panvad and Bodeli.

> Besides the traditional weapons like spears, '*palia*' and '*gophan*', this time the tribal used an innovative weapon. It could be referred to as an '*agni shastra*' - a 'fire bow', invented by attaching a rag soaked in fuel and setting it on fire seconds before shooting. The '*agni shastra*' wreaked havoc in Panvad and Kawant.
> 'They shot the "fire bows" at shops and houses, particularly those with heavy woodwork. Within minutes the targets were gutted,' said Deputy SP B L Parmar.

Another tactic attributed to the tribals is the use of poison-tipped bows. However, Parmar refused the theory that a typical tribal aggressor dips his bow in a poisonous concoction before sending it down the spine of his victim. 'The bow heads are rusted and hence infect the wound. This is normally misconstrued as poison to make the bows more [deadly]....', he said.

It is necessary to understand that guerrilla warfare is prompted by radical ideologies and is carried out over a long period of time in order to achieve ideological aims. The tribals in Panvad and Chhota Udepur have not developed any such ideology. To think of them as Naxalites will be a fatal mistake, because such a line of thought echoed in newspapers a hundred times may actually create a stereotype which will lead to creating a movement where none exists. The violence in Panvad is clearly a case of rioting by a generation that has come under great economic stress and has decided to adopt the moneylender as the role model. Militant tribal movements are always *against* the moneylenders and landlords. In the case of the Panvad riots, the drive was basically to emulate the Hindu moneylender; and, therefore, the wrath was directed against the Muslim moneylenders and not the institution of *sahukari*. This kind of apparent or perceived militancy can easily be mitigated by appropriate economic measures leading to a general development of tribals. If, on the other hand, it is handled without any understanding or compassion, it will acquire an undesirable tone.

4

Threatened Speech

I

In the case of the adivasi, the future is the enemy of the past. The forces of modernisation are rapidly wiping out adivasi cultural tradition. The economic marginalisation of the adivasis is seen as a result of something inherent in their traditions and social structures, and not a consequence of historical and legal interventions issuing out of colonialism. The ignorance about social structures, world-views and cultural practices of the adivasis is quite pervasive. We have not made even the slightest progress in the direction of understanding adivasi art and literature in India. Most of our literary critics and art historians remain innocent about the existence of adivasi art and literature. However, the art and literature of adivasi communities in India have their own peculiar identity. When we look at them as strangers, our response to them is trapped in quasi-anthropological parameters. Lacking the patience and inclination to understand them on their own terms, we hurriedly conclude that these are art forms of communities which have merely fallen out from mainstream Indian society and have remained frozen in some remote historical time. A careful study of adivasi arts and literature, however, indicates that this is not the case. Even within the field of Indian adivasi art, the variety is far too immense to admit a single definition or descriptive apparatus. Adivasi communities clearly show that there are distinctive features that separate the northeastern groups from the Himalayan groups and the mid-western groups.

One of the main characteristics of adivasi art is its peculiar manner of constructing space and imagery. This manner may be described, as 'hallucinatory'. Whether it is the oral and literary form of representation, or the visual and pictorial form, adivasi artists seem to interpret verbal and pictorial space as demarcated by an extremely flexible 'framing'. The boundaries, therefore, between art and non-art are highly porous. An adivasi epic can commence its narration almost out of a trivial everyday event. Adivasi paintings merge with their own living space as if the two are no different at all. And within the narrative itself, or within the painted imagery, there is no deliberate attempt made to follow a sequence. The episodes retold and the images created take on the apparently chaotic shapes of dreams. In an adivasi *Ramayana*, one can find a sudden and surprising appearance of an episode from the *Mahabharata*. In their paintings, one can find a curious mixture of traditional and modern imagery. Yet, one would be wrong in assuming that adivasi arts do not employ any ordering principles. On the contrary, there are very strict ordering principles. The most important among these is 'tradition'. Though a casual spectator does not notice it, every adivasi performance and creation has, as a pre-text, another such performance or creation belonging to a previous occasion. The creativity of adivasi artists lies in adhering to the past and at the same time slightly but definitely subverting it. The subversions are, however, more playful than ironic.

Playfulness, indeed, is the soul of adivasi art. Though oral and pictorial art creations in adivasi communities are intimately related to ritual, and though the element of the sacred can never be left out of creativity, adivasi art is rarely pompous, nor does it assume a moralising tone. The artist very seldom, if at all, plays the role of the creator. Listening to adivasi epics can be great fun because even the heroes are not spared the occasional shock of the artist's humour. One reason for this unique mixture of the sacred and the ordinary in adivasi arts may be that they are not created with the specific objective of sale. One must, however, never forget that even amongst the adivasis, artists do expect a certain amount of patronage from the community. Very often the persons performing the rituals are themselves artists. There is no element of competition involved in the patron-artist relationship. Adivasi arts, therefore, are relaxed and not tense.

One more distinctive feature of adivasi art is its indulgence of the medium. When an adivasi storyteller narrates an episode, he likes to stop at a phrase or word, and play upon its tonal qualities exploiting the most out of its phonetic potential. Adivasi craftsmen and painters like to show off their love of the colours they use. They have an intense sense of shapes and figures and an acute feel for the texture of the materials that they use. In whatever they build or make, they know how to reveal and highlight the shapes, tones and textures that they handle. It is as if for them the message of the medium is far more important than the message framed in the conceptual understanding of the artist. Hence, every adivasi artist conceals his individual identity by foregrounding the medium itself. Adivasi creations exude a certain love for the materials used, almost as if they are prayerful offerings to the elements that make this world such a mysteriously beautiful place.

One question that is invariably asked in the context of adivasi art is whether they are static and frozen in tradition forever or whether they keep growing. There is a general misconception about oral art traditions that they are far too tradition-bound and that they do not leave much scope for individual experimentation beyond the little freedom to deviate from the previously created text. This misconception arises out of the notion that art has to be seen only with reference to the text. But in reality, art is much more than the text. It involves performance as well as the audience's reception. Experimentation in adivasi art can be understood only when it is approached as performative art.

Adivasis do have an immense capacity to assimilate outside influences. They have highly evolved mechanisms of responding to the non-adivasi world. Usually one forgets to notice that all adivasi communities in India are basically bilingual. And all bilingual communities in the world possess an innate capacity to handle influences and to assimilate them. The oral stories and songs of the adivasis employ this bilingualism in such a complex manner that a linguist who is not alert to this complexity may tend to dismiss the very existence of their languages as dialects of our major languages.

II

Nobody today asks the question 'What is literature?' There was a time when this question was asked and attempts were made to provide an answer. Thinkers have realised, however, that every answer to this question is but partial. The reason for our inability to provide a universally satisfactory answer to this question is that the notions of literature change from age to age and from culture to culture. Therefore, one merely points to various answers that other thinkers have provided and to the inadequacies in those answers. One points out that literature is not a concept belonging to the same category of concepts as 'matter' which somehow can be defined with at least a degree of certitude. Rather, it is a concept like 'truth' which invites discussion of other concepts such as 'reality' and 'perception' before it can be tackled.

For a long time literature was tagged on to 'beauty', 'experience', 'grace', and also to concepts involving mental processes such as 'creativity', 'imagination' and 'inspiration'. It has also been enlisted in describing the materiality of language in terms of 'style' and 'structure'. Obviously, the notions of literature discussed by different thinkers are based on a variety of experiences, each of which may have been recognised and identified as 'literary experience' by the respective thinker.

In our time 'literary experience' has become synonymous with the experience of the written word. Those of us who think of literature and speak about it have developed an unduly high degree of reverence for the written word. First printing technology contributed to the rise of this sentiment. Then the influence of colonisation on cultures outside Europe gave it the status of a science or a 'form of knowledge'. More recently, developments in the field of linguistics and structuralism, and their impact on philosophical debate, have made discussion on speech, without any reference to writing, almost impossible.

However, there are times in the history of a culture when one has to look upon sophisticated philosophical discussions as an expensive luxury. Had Aristotle found his brother dying in the middle of a battlefield or a street, I do not think he would have sat back and analysed death in terms of comedy and tragedy. If an Algerian youth from Derrida's neighbourhood had been picked up by the French police and had appealed to him for help, I do not think the philosopher would have thought of the appeal in terms of the intricate binds between the written and the spoken. Of course, it is necessary to be philosophical in times of war; but it is much more important to be *aware* that it is a philosophical exercise. Therefore, even if it is sheer madness to revive the question 'What is literature?', I would like to dispossess myself of all the rich heritage of philosophical thought relating to this question accumulated through the centuries, and take it up again, not out of naivete and certainly not out of arrogance towards the two great traditions—Western and Indian—of literary philosophy that are ready to lend me a helping hand. I want to return to this question so that the hypothetical brother of Aristotle dying in a Greek street and the hypothetical Algerian neighbour of Derrida tortured by the French police do not vanish altogether as a reference from the world of literary philosophy.

In India a vast number of languages have yet remained only spoken languages, and, as a result, literary compositions in these languages are not considered to be 'literature'. They are, of course, a feast for a folklorist, an anthropologist or a linguist; but for a literary critic these mean nothing. Similarly, there are several nomadic communities in India that are broken up and spread over long distances but have survived as communities because they are bound together through the tradition of their oral epics. The wealth and variety of these works is so enormous, it is with a sense of shame that one discovers their neglect. I recently discovered for myself an entire novel in the Bhili language (*Telav naa Mele*), an autobiographical narrative in the Goud Banjara language (*Tanda*), an epic in the Dangi language (*Satimaataa ni Katha*) and several plays conceived in the Bhantu language (spoken by the Sansis). These reminded me of the songs and stories I had heard during my childhood from itinerant street singers and which are not to be heard now.

For some years now I have been collecting songs and stories circulating in India's adivasi languages. I am overwhelmed by their number and their profound influence on the adivasi communities. The result is that I am no longer prepared to think of literature as something written. Of course, I do not want to dispute the claim that written compositions and texts have the status of literature; but surely it is time we realise that unless we modify the established notion of literature as the written, we will be silently witnessing the decline of a rich heritage of India's oral traditions. That literature is a lot more than writing is a reminder necessary for our times.

III

While the literary tradition in India is about 3500 years old, the practice of putting literary texts in the medium of print is barely 200 years old. India learnt about printing from the Portuguese in the seventeenth century; but it was not until the British started using the printing machine for the production of texts during the nineteenth century in India, that Indian literature was influenced by the new technology. The principal mode of literary transmission prior to the nineteenth century was oral. This is not to say that all compositions were entirely oral. Scripts had been used in India for recording literary and non-literary texts at least from the fifth century before Christ. Poets recorded their texts, using the known scripts, on thin barks of trees or palm leaves. Scholars who studied these texts and used them for teaching in schools and universities, reproduced them periodically so as to keep the written word alive. India learnt about paper technology in the twelfth century; and paper was used widely for the purpose of recording compositions. Multiple copies of such compositions were made using paper. And, yet the oral tradition was never completely replaced by the tradition of written literature.

The poetics of composition as well as the conventions of literary reception were profoundly influenced throughout the history of India by the orality of literature. Of the two major epics that have shaped Indian sensibility, the *Mahabharata* is an oral epic. So were the Puranas in their initial phase. The Suta used to narrate these orally. They gave to the common people religious and ethical instruction in the form of stories retold from the great epics. This convention of suta-narration came to an end some time during the ninth century. However, even today, every Indian village has an elder, a man or a woman, who performs the function of keeping the epic alive through the oral mode. Unlike the *Mahabharata*, the *Ramayana* was composed by a single author and in a uniform metre. The plot and the characters of the *Ramayana* show unity and consistency. Yet, even this epic was assimilated in the suta tradition of oral narration; and it became a common practice to listen to a learned man narrate the epic to devoted groups of Rama-lovers rather than read the poem itself.

The oral convention grew in range and variety as time passed. In ancient and medieval India, a number of oral forms of presentation developed around the plot of the *Ramayana*. The famous Ramalila, a form of ritual folk dance-drama depicts scenes from the *Ramayana*. And in every small and big town in north India, there are groups of local actors who produce the Ramalila even today. Some of the medieval translations of the *Ramayana* in modern Indian languages were meant more for oral transmission than for lexical accomplishment. Among these, the most notable is the *Tulsi-Ramayana*, a composition with which every speaker of the Hindi language has some familiarity. It must be added that the *Mahabharata* and the *Ramayana* were not appropriated entirely by the oral tradition. They made an equally significant contribution to the tradition of written literature in India. Kalidasa's celebrated literary work, *Raghuvamsha*, is the best known example of mainstream literature using the epics. One may, thereforc, say that the two epics functioned as the unifying link between the elite and the folk.

Why were the epics so perfectly assimilated into the oral tradition? In order to seek an answer to this question one must go back in history to the vedic period. The earliest known literary work in India is the *Rkveda* (or *Rigveda* as it is pronounced). This veda is considered to be authorless, *apaurusheya*, as if it was whispered into the ears of the vedic visionaries by gods and goddesses. The verses of this veda represent the sensibility of the earliest Aryan tribes who settled in India. Their compositions speak of man's primordial relation with nature and the mysteries surrounding nature. These verses were handed down the generations orally. In fact, they were composed in such a manner that they could be easily committed to memory. This manner of composition determined the nature of prosody in India. Some of the metres used in vedic poetry are in use even today, and they have been used throughout the span of 3500 years since their first invention.

The musical element in the vedic verses was so overpowering that the verses were believed to be vested with extraordinary magical powers. Having acquired this special spiritual status, vedic verses acquired a hold over the Indian imagination which the turbulent social history of India has not been able to shake off. In the course of time, the schools that taught vedic sciences developed special methods of memorising the verses. Books were written about the ways in which the oral purity of the mantras could be preserved. To this day vedic verses are transmitted orally and there are scholars who can recite the entire body of this ancient poetry without the slightest change of a syllable and exactly in the original oral form. Rarely has any other oral tradition of poetry been so venerated and so well preserved as the vedic tradition. It was because this tradition was already well established when the epics were composed that the epics too were committed to the oral tradition. In the mantra tradition, orality was employed to preserve the purity of the sacred, in the suta tradition it was used to achieve effectiveness of communication. In either case, the oral was privileged over the written.

Though poetry is easier to remember than prose, the oral tradition in Indian literature was by no means confined only to poetic literature. The Indian narrative tradition is moulded to suit orality from the very beginning of narrative fiction in India. The stories in the *Kathasaritasagara* and the *Jataka* stories reveal that they are structured for oral transmission by wandering monks. The stories themselves are never without the motif of a long journey; they are stories that have travelled and gathered more stories around them on the way. In these stories the plot moves from one character to another, one life to another, one place to another quite effortlessly. They were never constricted by the idea of unity of place, time and theme. They were stories to be told and retold, flexible in plot and accessible to audiences varying in social, religious and ethical persuasions. The well-defined conventions of gesture and the over-simplified story structure were favoured by Bharata, which indicates that there had been before him a long tradition of folk performances. Of course, in the course of time, dramatic texts were produced by Shudraka, Kalidasa, Bhavabhuti and Harsha. But never was a play written in ancient India which did not make use of folk elements and folk dialects. On the other hand, the folk forms of drama in India drew freely upon elite conventions, theology, philosophy and poetry. These forms continue to survive in most languages. The Kannada language has the Yakshagana theatre, the Gujarati language has the Bhavai theatre and Marathi has the Tamasha theatre. These are by no means primitive forms of drama. They are extremely sophisticated in technique and performance. Western dramatists and thinkers like Antonin Artaud and Bertolt Brecht have felt attracted to the techniques of combining mimesis and semiosis developed by Indian folk theatre. These regional forms do not have a fixed and written text to support the performance. They are spontaneous and depend on improvisation by the actors. And for that reason, they are closer to the audiences than plays with written texts.

Indian literature witnessed a great change at the beginning of the medieval period. From about the eleventh century to about the fifteenth century several new languages emerged in India as literary languages. These were derived from Sanskrit and Tamil and were languages commonly spoken by the people. It was about the same time that India started using paper for writing; the poets composing in the new languages had to develop the practice of composing texts that were at once written and oral. The poems were written, and copies of the written text were made, but the reproduction of these texts was done mainly through oral modes. It was for this reason that the diction of poetry was drawn from the spoken language and the concerns reflected in poetry were mainly the concerns of the people.

Previously, written literature in India depended for inspiration on literary conventions. From the eleventh century onward the lived life became more important for the poets. New modes of music and new metrical patterns started dominating poetry. Some of the very best poets in the history of Indian poetry - Nanak, Tukaram, Kabir, Mira, Akka Mahadevi, Narsi Mehta and Surdas - belong to this glorious period of Indian oral literature. These poets are collectively known as the bhakti poets, for they sang of a devotion that posed a challenge to established theology and social structure. They humanised god, brought religion to the people and brought people closer to religion. They worked as prophets of equality and freedom. But, above all, they created a poetry of abiding beauty in the languages spoken by the people, and in creating it, they created new literary languages. The influence of the bhakti poets on the Indian masses was so profound and pervasive that even to this day their songs are sung by people in villages and cities.

In Maharashtra, millions of people from all walks of life join in a pilgrimage twice every year to the temple-town of Pandharpur. As they walk there they sing the poems composed by Jnaneshwara (thirteenth century), Eknath (fifteenth century) and Tukaram (seventeenth century). The entire body of songs consists of hundreds of medieval poems learnt orally. Similarly, the poems of Mira, Nanak and Kabir are learnt orally and sung by millions of Indians to this day. These poems are so intricately entwined with the consciousness of the Indian masses that they can hardly be separated from the thought processes. Though meant for the masses and dominated by music that made the lines and verses easy to remember, the medieval bhakti poetry had an amazing range and depth of philosophic, social and moral concerns.

Bhakti poetry was oral in practice but of remarkable aesthetic sophistication and philosophic maturity. Besides, it was poetry that brought about social integration as all great literature does. It cut across the barriers of caste, religion, gender and age. And, finally, it performed the valuable task of bringing the heritage of ancient Indian culture to modern India.

The use of paper for writing had become common practice

during the seventeenth century. And the poets, chroniclers and storytellers felt encouraged to write their works in decorated books because they could then get royal patronage. During this century and the next, a process of canon building began in Indian literature, a process by which the written work was considered more valuable than an oral composition. The force behind this new canon building was Islam which held the written word to be sacred. Calligraphy became a precious art, and book making became a common practice. Hence, the transition from calligraphy to printing was extremely smooth. This transition took place during the nineteenth century.

It was during the nineteenth century again that literature became a subject taught in schools and universities on a mass scale. Whenever literature becomes a subject taught in schools and universities, its manifestation in the form of written books is valued more than its orality. Gradually, literary scholarship forgets the fact that the use of written books in classrooms is merely a matter of convenience, and it starts looking upon oral literature as literature with some deficiency. When the written word acquires totemic importance, the spoken word is seen as taboo. This happened in India too. However it was only in the institutions of literary education that oral literature was seen as a sign of cultural backwardness. The ancient and medieval literary traditions continued to be handed down from one to the next generation through oral means. Perhaps it is this love for the oral that has brought cinema to the centre of modern India's cultural life. Indian cinema, which is crowded with songs and descriptive passages more than narrative sequences is more akin to Indian oral literature than to the cinema of the western world. However, in order to understand oral literature in India during the twentieth century one must turn to an altogether different area of expression—that of the adivasi languages.

The Indian Constitution recognises some of the major literary languages as the national languages of India. The national academy of letters, the Sahitya Akademi, recognises a few more in addition to those recognised by the Constitution. But in addition to these, there are nearly 88 other languages in India which are spoken by a large number of people. According to the census of 1971, each of these 88 languages is spoken by at least 10,000 people. These languages are termed 'adivasi', but they are not primitive or half-developed languages. Most of them have literary traditions that are oral. Scholars studying these languages have observed that they have developed their independent poetics and literary conventions.

Recently a new interest in these oral literatures in India is emerging in the literary community. A little over a decade ago, the noted poet and anthropologist A.K. Ramanujan published a collection of folk stories in India. His stories show how well structured adivasi narratives can be. A similar attempt was made by Kanaji Patel, the young editor of *Gadyaparva*, a literary magazine in Gujarati. Kanaji Patel, a poet and novelist himself, observed that in the adivasi tradition of oral narratives there is no alienation between the narrator and what is being narrated. Just as the adivasis know how to put the entire physical body to use in daily life, they know how to employ the entire body of language for literary expression.

Dr. Bhagwandas Patel is another Gujarati scholar who has drawn the attention of the literary community to oral literature. He has published the written versions of oral narratives and epics such as *Bhilonu Bharath* and *Gujarona Arela* composed by the Bhil adivasis. In grandeur of conception and the magic of their effect they are comparable to any epic in the world. In other areas of India, mainly Rajasthan, Madhya Pradesh, Karnataka and Maharashtra, the adivasis continue their own traditions of long narrative poems through oral transmission. In the same way, they continue their own traditions of theatre. One of the most talented of Indian directors, Habib Tanvir, has brought to light the great elan with which the adivasis from Chhattisgarh perform in theatre. The productions of Habib Tanvir, the epics recorded by Bhagwandas Patel, the narratives collected by Kanaji Patel, the stories retold by A.K.Ramanujan and all such other works go to show that the oral traditions of literature in India are as active as the traditions of written literature. Moreover, they are less marked by the influence of the colonising west, and, to that extent, are closer to the spirit of Indian culture and tradition. Adivasi languages, therefore, have a claim to their rightful place of importance in Indian literature.

IV

One of the most significant features of Indian civilisation is its immense linguistic variety. Given that languages show marked variations in their phonological behaviour from one geographical region to another, it is but natural that a vast geographical expanse such as India should give rise to a large variety of dialects. But not all large countries have such a variety as India has. This is so mainly because of India's peculiar history of assimilation of different cultures during the course of the last three millennia. The result is that, with its wealth of more than twenty written languages and over a thousand dialects, India is today a unique 'linguistic field'.

For any nation state in the world, it becomes necessary to regulate the growth and development of languages in order to keep the country together and at the same time to do proper justice to the nature and identity of its linguistic heritage. This problem had been a part of the thinking that went into the drafting of India's Constitution which provides the foundation for various policies for cultural development in independent India. There were debates during the pre-independence days as to which language could be made the national language, which one the language of administration, and in how many languages could literary programmes be initiated. As a result, the makers of our Constitution decided to include a special schedule of languages. In this, the 8th Schedule, Hindi was listed as the national language; but provision was also made for English to perform that function for a limited period of ten years. Thirteen other languages were included as the languages of administration. The reason for not including other languages was that it would be impractical to run the business of the government and the judiciary in each and every language. Subsequently, through Constitutional amendments, three more languages were added to the 8th Schedule. The other statutory bodies which had to deal with languages and literature followed, more or less, the principles laid down in the Constitution; but they added to this list a few more as and when the need was felt. Thus the Sahitya Akademi and the National Book Trust have been publishing books in twenty-two languages.

But there is another beginning to the story of the development of modern Indian languages. In order to trace it one must go back to the eleventh century. The cultural forms developed in classical India from the third to the tenth centuries started undergoing momentous changes at the beginning of the last millennium. The most fundamental of these was the emergence of new languages - *bhashas* - all over the Indian subcontinent. The new *bhashas* expressed regional and heterodox aspirations in protest against the hegemony of Sanskrit and the culture developed through that language, *sanskriti.* A similar movement occurred in the south with respect to Tamil which, after a continuous history of two thousand years, branched into Telugu (eleventh century). Earlier, Kannada had already become an independent dialect of Tamil (fifth century). Nine hundred years later, Tamil and Kannada jointly gave birth to Malayalam (fourteenth century). In the north, the regional dialects known as Apabhramsha asserted themselves as independent languages. Consequently, the Middle Indo-Aryan dialect in the east split into Bangla and Oriya (tenth century). Subsequently, Bangla gave birth to Assamiya (thirteenth century). The northwestern dialect developed into Kashmiri (thirteenth century), Sindhi (fifteenth century) and Punjabi (fifteenth century). The western Apabhramsha of Middle Indo-Aryan distributed itself into Hindi (which till the beginning of the nineteenth century existed as several distinct dialects), Gujarati (eleventh century) and Marathi (eleventh century). The Hindi family of dialects developed autonomy in the fourteenth century. It also interacted with the Islamic languages. There were Persian, which was spoken in India from the thirteenth to nineteenth centuries, and Arabic, in use from the eleventh to the nineteenth centuries. This interaction of Hindi with Persian and Arabic produced a cantonment language, Urdu (thirteenth century), which later became a great literary language.

The origin of some of these languages can be traced further back to earlier centuries. We are told that Gujarati and Marathi, for example, existed in rudimentary forms as found in stray inscriptions and isolated verses dating from the eighth century. Their known literary traditions, however, do not seem to emerge until a century or two after each language assumed a distinct identity. In any case, all *bhashas* became literary languages by the end of the fifteenth century. These literary traditions survived two phases of prolonged alien rule; and many of them have claims to a large number of great literary works and major authors. The emergence and survival of mature literary traditions in so many languages is the greatest phenomenon in Indian cultural history.

During the last quarter of the eighteenth century, the question of Indian languages attracted the attention of the colonial rulers. Those who were translating from Indian languages, mainly Sanskrit and Persian, started applying the principles of comparative philology to the mass of languages accessible to them. The most important among these scholars was Sir William Jones. He found remarkable similarities between Sanskrit and other classical languages such as Greek and Latin. He concluded that all these had probably developed from a common source. Under the influence of the orientalist scholars, a new philosophy of historical linguistics developed in Germany and France which started classifying human languages into language-families. Initially, it was claimed that all Indian languages had grown out of Sanskrit. Gradually, the Dravidic family was noticed, the source of which was Tamil. But subsequent researches, mostly during the twentieth century, have indicated that there are at least five major language-families in India: (1) Indo-European (a) Indo-Aryan; (b) Germanic; (2) Dravidian; (3) Austro-Asiatic; (4) Tibeto-Burmese; (5) Semito-Hamitic. All the languages listed in the 8th Schedule of the Constitution belong to the first two families, and those that are not listed belong mostly to the remaining three families. The classification of Indian languages as made at present in terms of families is as follows:

1. **Indo-European**

(a) Indo-Aryan:

(1) Assamese (s)	(2) Bengali(s)	(3) Bhili/Bhilodi
(4) Bishnupuriya	(5) Dogri	(6) Gujarati(s)
(7) Halabi	(8) Hindi(s)	(9) Kashmiri(s)
(10) Khandeshi	(11) Konkani(s)	(12) Lahnada
(13) Marathi(s)	(14) Nepali(s)	(15) Oriya(s)

(16) Punjabi(s) (17) Sanskrit(s) (18) Sindhi(s)
(19) Urdu(s)

(b) Germanic:
(1) English.

2. **Dravidian**

(1) Coorgi/Kodagu (2) Gondi (3) Jatapu
(4) Kannada(s) (5) Khond/Kondh (6) Kisan
(7) Kolami (8) Konda (9) Koya
(10) Kui (11) Kurukh/Oraon
(12) Malayalam(s) (13) Malto (14) Parji
(15) Tamil(s) (16) Telugu(s) (17) Tulu

3. **Austro-Asiatic**

(1) Bhumij (2) Gadaba (3) Ho
(4) Juang (5) Kharia (6) Khasi
(7) Koda/Kora (8) Korku (9) Korwa
(10) Munda (11) Mundari
(12) Nicobarese (13) Santali (14) Savara

4. **Tibeto-Burmese**

(1) Adi (2) Anal (3) Angami
(4) Ao (5) Bhotia
(6) Bodo/Boro (7) Chakesang
(8) Chakru/Chokri (9)Chang (10) Deori
(11) Dimasa (12) Gangte (13) Garo
(14) Halam (15) Hmar (16) Kabul
(17) Karbi/Mikir (18) Khezha
(19) Khiemnungan (20) Kinnauri (21) Koch
(22) Kom (23) Konyak (24) Kuki
(25) Lahuli (26) Lakher (27) Lalung
(28) Lepcha (29) Liangmei (30) Limbu
(31) Lotha (32) Lushai/Mizo
(33) Manipuri(s) (34) Mao (35) Maram
(36) Maring (37) Miri/Mishing (38) Mishmi
(39) Mogh (40) Monpa

(41) Nissi/Dafla	(42) Nocte	(43) Paite
(44) Pawl	(45) Phom	(46) Pochury
(47) Rabha	(48) Rengma	(49) Sangtam
(50) Sema	(51) Sherpa	(52) Tangkhul
(53) Tangsa	(54) Thado	(55) Tibetan
(56) Tripuri	(57) Vaiphei	(58) Wancho
(59) Yimchungre	(60) Zeliang	(61) Zemi
(62) Zou		

5. Semito-Hamitic

(1) Arabic / Arbi

However, this neat separation of languages in theory does not accurately reflect the ground reality of the language field. In order to get a picture of that, one must look into the figures provided by the census. These figures show that the languages listed in the 8th Schedule have a much larger number of speakers than those not included. The only exception to this is that of English. This increase is caused not only by the general population growth in different linguistic states but also by the decline of the languages not included in the Schedule. This decline is natural (and probably expected) by the policy makers, because the facilities provided for language education are only for the languages included in the 8th Schedule. In the years to come the other languages, mostly spoken by adivasi communities and belonging to the Austro-Asiatic family and the Tibeto-Burmese family may disappear altogether as a demographic indicator. That is to say that while the diction and the syntax patterns of these languages will no doubt survive, there may be a greater assimilation of these in the main languages of India. Whether this is desirable or not is a question that cultural anthropologists will have to answer.

As for the main languages, the picture of their development is a mixed one. On the one hand, there is an unprecedented growth in the printed materials in these languages, and naturally so considering the multiplication of the print capitalism in the twentieth century. But on the other hand, the English language has come up as the major adversary to these languages. Many members of the class, which during the nineteenth century advocated the cause of an Indian language, have turned to English as a medium for their personal economic betterment. As such, there has been a sharp decline in the number of readers of literature in Indian languages in cities and semi-urban areas. On the other hand, the phenomenal spread of formal education in India's vast rural areas has provided a new generation of readers and authors of Indian languages. In the process, new dialect varieties have entered the main stream of Indian languages. The figures entered in the 1991 Census Report under the category of mother tongues are as follows, with respect to the scheduled languages:

S.No.	*Language*	*No. of speakers*	*Percentage*
1.	Hindi	33,72,72,114	37.50
2.	Bengali	6,95,95,738	8.22
3.	Telugu	6,60,17,615	7.80
4.	Marathi	6,24,81,681	7.38
5.	Tamil	5,34,06,932	5.13
6.	Urdu	4,34,06,932	5.13
7.	Gujarati	4,06.73,814	4.81
8.	Kannada	3,27,53,676	3.87
9.	Malayalam	3,03,77,176	3.59
10.	Oriya	2,80,61,313	3.32
11.	Punjabi	2,33,78,744	2.76
12.	Assamese	1,30,79,696	1.55
13.	Sindhi	21,22,848	0.25
14.	Nepali	20,76,645	0.25
15.	Konkani	17,60,607	0.21
16.	Manipuri	12,70,216	0.15
17.	Kashmiri	not available	not available
18.	Sanskrit	49,736	0.01

These figures indicate that Hindi is now claimed as the mother tongue by almost one in every three Indians. However, it is necessary to bear in mind that what is counted as Hindi is in reality a group of a large number of dialects, regional varieties and sub-languages. Hindi was claimed as the mother tongue by 20.85 crores of the population in 1971, and by 26.45 crores in 1981. This rise in number almost equals the total of Bengali speakers (7 crores). As against Hindi which is the most widely spoken language in India, Sindhi, Nepali, Konkani, Manipuri, Kashmiri and Sanskrit, other languages listed in the schedule, together do not have more than 0.75 crores of speakers. Leaving these two uneven ends of the spectrum, the remaining eleven languages (Assamese, Bengali, Gujarati, Malayalam, Marathi, Kannada, Oriya, Punjabi, Tamil and Urdu) are spoken by almost half the population of India. Thus, these figures clearly show that there is a five-fold structure of Indian languages in terms of development. At the top are Hindi and English as growing languages. Next come the other major literary languages such as Bengali, Oriya, Marathi, Tamil, Kannada, Punjabi, etc. Though the census lists Urdu in this group, the precise relation between Urdu and Hindi needs to be investigated in order to decide the distinction between their identities. After this is the group of major languages with a relatively smaller number of speakers, — languages such as Sindhi, Manipuri, Konkani, etc. At the tail end of this structure can be placed two other groups: the first a group of languages that are not recognised as separate from the main language though there is some justification for that recognition. These include languages like Kachchi, Ahirani, Marwadi, etc. In the second group are the languages of adivasi communities and communities that are nomadic. A language like Bhantu, which is spoken by the Kanjars, Sansis, Chharas, and such other semi-nomadic groups, or Bhilli, which is spoken by nearly 0.3 crores, stands no chance of development because there are likely to be no schools or colleges teaching these languages, and no printing will ever be attempted in them. Thus in this five-fold structure, the languages on the higher rungs are developed at the cost of languages on the lower rungs.

V

Experience accumulates. Then it stabilises in cognition with verbal forms, or even a pre-verbal but conscious sensation. These verbal forms are exchanged and transacted among the members of a community. Such transactions make the community possible as well. The two are interdependent. Over a period of time, people discover, borrow and in some rare instances invent methods of recording the cognition, as well as systems of representation, such as orthography. Orthography is an expensive affair, it has been so all along. It takes several years for a person to acquire command over the rules and the restlessness of systems of representation. Therefore, records of human cognition easily tend to become the monopoly of a certain class that has the ability to buy leisure for the young ones so that they can 'learn'. This is where human learning and the 'learning' in a classroom part ways. History shows that classroom learning generates its own rhetoric to justify the sanctity of its superior cognitive content, more systematic than vulgar sensory experience. But in fact, vulgar sensory experience is the basis of all human knowledge. Subsequently, this rhetoric acquires the status of the basic principles in knowledge-systems such as logic, rationality, veracity, and so on. Human history is, in a way, a story of conflict between learning and experience, between the rational and the imaginative, between the left and the right halves of the brain. Knowledge, therefore, is a way of repression, and hence, while examining the knowledge-systems of the adivasis, one has to define, with some clarity at least, what knowledge means, and what it means to think of it as a system.

5

Language and Reality

The process of human evolution holds many secrets. We understand so little about it. Our inadequate understanding leads us to build apparently scientific hypotheses. But these hypotheses are such that even the exactly contrary hypotheses sound equally convincing. Language as a social institution, the nature of its exact origin, and the clear sequence in its formation are some of the mysteries in the epic text of human evolution.

Was there an attendant sound when the universe came into existence? Did sound exist at all prior to the animal ability to perceive sound? Do the eternal sound — the *anahat dhvani* — and the sound by vocal cords belong to the same material type? Why did the human animal select regulation of breath by the vocal chords as the means for meaning - transaction, while through the eyes, or through body movement (as with honey bees) the meaning transaction might have been equally effective? Why did the human animal not cultivate those other means of expression with equal degree of obsession? All these questions can be answered at a theoretical level; but the answers do not cross the level of philosophical propositions that are true but at the same time not entirely untrue. Regulation of air by the vocal chords came to be the central mode of meaning transaction, subsequently numericals and letters became surrogates for sound. Why did not then the script language entirely displace the sound language? While the theory of language acquisition inherent in the psychic structure of an infant has been formulated, why is that no theory as yet been postulated regarding the natural ability to perceive the correspondence between those geometrical shapes called letters and the human sounds called syllables?

'Meaning' consists of the meaning expressed through gesticulations, sound - regulation and script marks as well as through the silence and stillness outside the pale of these three. Therefore, what exactly constitutes 'meaning' has not been conclusively determined. At the most, the theories of meaning have remained at the level of philosophical speculation. Besides, it has not been possible so far to state with any great precision as to whether meaning is language, or if meaning exists prior to language, is yet another social or metaphysical system completely independent of verbal language, and is capable of transcending human language. It is true that language as an experiential phenomenon is within the range of an individual's perception, but it is also true that an individual's ability to perceive the world is conditioned by verbal language. This has led us to conclude that language is a social institution.

But is language 'meaning', or is it some material 'thing'? Is it a transcendental energy or a purely social institution? Or is it a mere biological function given to the human body in the process of evolution? Or is it all of these at once or in various aspects of the language phenomenon? All these questions need to be tackled fully despite linguistics being the most developed among the human sciences.

There is a well-established view that culture has no other expression but language, that the two are one and the same. It is maintained that cognition too would be impossible without language. A similar view on meaning too exists. In other words, 'language' has been used as a synonym for that which determines the outer boundaries of each transaction of the human intelligence.

Even when the structure of dreams is not based on language content, it is conceptualised as being the same as language structure; the origin of dreams is in the ability to remember, in memory. In other words we are made to believe that memory cannot exist entirely in absence of language. Similarly, we have come to believe that other psychic possibilities such as inspiration, imagination and reason cannot exist in the absence of language.

While these hypotheses seem unexceptionable, it is true that there are experiences that the human animal shares with others animals that show a marked absence of language based on sound regulation. Vertigo, or the fear of falling, and love or sensuous attraction are the main instances of such experiences.

Phenomenology, which is one of the sciences of human understanding, maintains that language develops 'in tune' with the perpetually increasing scope of the phenomenon perceived by the human mind. As against this, it has been argued that the human grasp of the phenomenal reality increases in proportion to the ever-increasing ability of language to grasp complexities. It is indeed difficult to establish if a domain of experience exists independently and outside the domain of language. At the same time it is even more difficult to over rule the existence of such a domain of experience.

Similarly complicated is the question whether those semi-verbal or verbal substances that scripts, grammars and cultures do not admit as language, are language or not? At best they find a place in marginal categories such as dialects and regional varieties. In fact, in the vast spectrum of meaning beginning with the mysterious origin of sound, to its pervasive spread through human space and time, human languages may at best be seen as dialects of the uninterrupted *dhvani.* Similarly, in the total range of meaning capable of being conducted through material and symbolic means, the sound-symbol based language will have to be counted as a dialect of the total range of meaning.

Moreover, the process of the perpetual enlargement and deepening of our understanding of the world indicates the possibility that, perhaps, the language-substance known to us at the present stage of our evolution is but a partial fraction of the ultimate possibilities of the meaning substance available to the human senses. Therefore, in some ways language will have to be thought of as a part, as a dialect, of the totality of experience. And the totality of the human languages stabilised through words and scripts will have to be seen as a dialect of the totality of all experience, all meaning and all sound as a simple entity. Therefore to be a dialect is not to be left behind but to be the avant-garde.

One can understand the true nature of dialect if one conceptualises it as a necessary component, not as a decaying remnant, of language whose destiny it is to be at the turbulent interface of an ever-expanding reality, to be the 'advance party' for grasping untapped frontiers of meaning. Histories of languages show that it has been their fate to keep catching up with the dialects, not the other way round. The destiny of dialects is to persist in their exploration of new possibilities of meaning, albeit without losing their relationship with the standardised languages to which they are bound by political and historical circumstances. The destiny of a dialect is to remain in currency but, unfortunately, with the value of the counterfeit.

To use a metaphor, dialect is like the amorphous substance surrounding a newly born planet, which is yet to find its ultimate rate of revolution. That planet environment of the language is defined by its dialects. It is through them that language keeps its ceaseless contact with the universe outside it, and therefore manages to belong to it.

So far it has been maintained that the speech variety of the dominant class acquires the status of the standard language, whereas the speech varieties of the dominated are seen as dialects. This view is based on the history of the English language in England. But going by this logic the Hindi spoken by the politically dominant Indians should have by now become the standard variety of Hindi, and the Marathi of the Maratha rulers should have become its main variety. The Indian experience indicates that the history of English in England does not provide enough scientific foundation for a universal dialectology. Besides, for cultures where the politically dominant class has often happened to be speaking a non-native language, and where the culturally dominant class has not been monolingual, dialects have to be thought about all over again.

Linguistics and Anthropology have co existed in the west for over two centuries with a close interdependence. Therefore, an equation between dialects and cultural disadvantage has come to be accepted.

If we set aside this questionable equation and postulate that language is a means of bringing the ever-expanding universe of experience within the grasp of human understanding, then it will follow that dialects (or sub-languages) have a place of primary importance in the process of internalisation of meaning for a given language.

In this process, it becomes necessary to achieve a meaningful amalgamation of new sensations with the most ancient memories. With a view to achieving this amalgamation, dialects put to stake their existence and identity, and bring to a given language an enriched sensitivity and ability to express.

A language without dialects will tend to become a meaningless heap of cliches. In such a situation words will become faceless and materials without personalities. Perhaps such a language might achieve, out of a grammatical purity, the power of perfect abstraction, as in mathematics. But the sound tokens in it will be so impersonal that they will alienate the 'animal' user, with a living consciousness, altogether.

A language must have a personality. Human beings will carry the burden of language only so long as they feel proud of belonging to their respective languages.

For centuries, European linguists have made attempts at tracing the one original language, the mother of all languages. At the back of these attempts was the myth of the Tower of Babel, the one original dispersed into innumerable imitations

It appears that each and every individual speaker in the human race is, from the first encounter with sound, engaged in the process of exploring every experience of the universe. Collectively, all of us have been trying to bring that experience into sound and in script whenever possible.

U. R. Anantha Murthy has often stated that the future of the Indian *bhashas* lies in the upkeep of their backyards. These backyards are really the sources of their being and growth. The dialects, sub-languages, language varieties and the backyard tongues are the energy that has kept the stream of Indian culture flowing for several millennia. To continue the metaphor of the stream, the so-called main languages are its banks; the dialects are the flow of the steam. To keep the streams going is the minimum that we should do.

6

Adivasi Knowledge and Aphasia

It is generally known that adivasis have their own knowledge traditions. But we do not know how to locate them. Sometimes we think that we may get the essential knowledge of tribals in their oral compositions. Accordingly we collect their stories and songs. But often this literature remains at the level of anthropological curiosity. Often a literary scholar or historian undertakes a serious study of the area, but begins to lose interest in its significance after some time. With respect to tribes like the Rathwas or the Saoras, we think we might find their knowledge systems in their paintings. But we cannot understand their symbolic system. Talking to adivasis we might get the feeling that they do not have any knowledge systems worth the name; but then, looking at the way they live, the way they build their houses, their understanding of nature, we cannot help concluding that they have a deep knowledge of things. Viewing the adivasi code of morals where there is no exploitation, little inequality, or gender discrimination, and where there is love for animals and nature, it may appear that the adivasis know much more than the non-adivasis. Yet, if we want to seek and understand their wisdom and knowledge, we do not know where to begin to look for it.

There are very few individuals among the adivasis who can or do speak about their own knowledge systems. It is as if some profound aphasia has gripped them. A few significant questions emerge from this: 1) what is knowledge? 2) What is aphasia? 3) What would be the most authentic way of representing the knowledge of the adivasis?

In order to find answers to such questions, I asked incessant questions of my adivasi friends in a two-day workshop at Baroda and Tejgadh. The workshop was held in February 1999 under the title 'The Future of the Adivasi Knowledge Systems'.

The writers and artists who participated in the long discussion mostly belong to Bhasha's collective of the *Dhol* magazine. Others were visiting scholars.

The participates in the discussion were:

1. Avaneesh Bhatt: Teacher of English, translator from adivasi bhashas
2. Ajay Dandekar, historian, social activist
3. Ramchandra Guha, a historian of modern India and biographer of Verrier Elwin
4. Rajendra Nanavati: An eminent professor of Sanskrit at Baroda University
5. Jayendra Soni: Indian professor of Sanskrit working in Germany
6. Luitgard Soni: A German psycho-speech therapist

The following adivasi scholars also participated:

1. Subhash Ishai
2. Subhash Pawara
3. Dhirubhai Patel
4. Atmaram Rathod
5. Chamulal Rathwa
6. Dahyabhai Vadhu
7. Shankarbhai Tadvi

Participating artists:

1. Mohanbhai: A Weaver
2. Kocharbhai Rathwa: A Painter and a Shaman
3. Mansinghbhai Rathwa: A Painter
4. Kodarbhai Varia: A Potter

Students were represented by
Naginbhai C. Rathwa

What follows is an accurate record of the discussion. It was recorded in writing in Marathi, Gujarati and English by three of my colleagues. The Gujarati version was subsequently included in my Gujarati book *Adivasi Jane Chhe* (The Adivasi Knows).

I began by asking Luitgard Soni, What is aphasia?

L. Soni : Yesterday, I met Dr Devy for the first time and during the conversation he mentioned the term aphasia. Actually, this is a medical term. It means loss of speech. This can occur due to an injury of the brain. There are several causes for it. For example, when there is a stroke or when there is an accident and the brain is injured. We have in the brain specific areas for the ability of speech and language. If any one of these several areas is destroyed, then we have aphasia. A medical model is used to interpret the above neurological matters. Based on this model, there are three types of aphasia:

1. *Sensory/perceptive aphasia:* The channel through which I hear and understand is the sensory perceptive channel. And if this is damaged, I will lose this ability. I will not be able to understand what is being said. There are two possibilities: a) I will not be able to decode words, the elements. I will therefore not be able to meaningfully decode the sequence. We have an area in the brain which can decode words and if this area is damaged it results in sensory or perceptive aphasia. b) If an individual loses this ability then he /she will fail to learn and use language meaningfully.
2. *Motoric aphasia:* This is the actual activity of speaking and pronouncing. The area in the brain where the order is given for motoric processes gets damaged here. The brain is responsible for our physical movements. Here, I cannot say or utter what I think; I cannot formulate words. For example, if I want to say 'cow' or 'elephant', I know this in the brain but my instruments of speech do not follow this. Thus the expressive channel is damaged. The result is motoric aphasia.

3. *Amnesic aphasia:* It is the problem where one cannot find the words one is looking for. It is similar to what happens to most of us at times - the word is at the tip of the tongue but we do not remember it.

These three types of aphasia can occur as a combination in a patient and can overlap. This is a model of aphasia for medical purposes. I think we can extend the meaning of aphasia in modern or post-modern societies as a loss of the ability to communicate. Even in medical terms, I can see this in society, a loss of understanding, of the ability to communicate with each other. For example, in my profession I see this loss of communication especially in children. But I can apply this to many strata of society.

To Dahyabhai Vadhu: The adivasis do not communicate the knowledge they have. Is this the reason why they are facing aphasia?

D. Vadhu: This knowledge about nature's secrets is known to a handful of people and so they have a grip over the community. The power of these secrets can be used for good purposes too. The Dangs Forest Department has attempted to document the knowledge of ethnomedicine but they have been able to document and publish only very primary knowledge. When they tried to discuss the tradition of soluble medicine, the Bhagats refused to disclose the processes because if this knowledge became public, there would be no difference between the ordinary people and the Bhagats. They wanted to maintain this difference and keep the knowledge to themselves.

There are secret methods to collect medicine. Care has to be taken while plucking the herbs. For instance, while plucking herbs, the shadow of the herb-collector should not fall on the plant. Or again the plant may have to be plucked at a particular time during the day — in the morning, afternoon or evening. But the Bhagats do not reveal this, as they want to keep it within the family. There are agricultural methods, like burning leaves before farming, which everyone knows. This knowledge percolates to everyone. For example, the underground source of water in the land can be known from the trees growing there. Where there are *umbar* trees, there, surely, is water. Those who are interested know these methods. They do not turn this knowledge into disciplines, but only those who are interested learn these.

To Atmaram Kaniram Rathod : Tribals are facing aphasia. What do you have to say in this regard on behalf of the Banjara community?

A.K. Rathod: Though adivasis have a lot of knowledge, the reason for this loss of voice is the attack of urban society on them. They have very good understanding of space and direction. The *shivling* is one of the manifestations, one of the discoveries of tribals. It works like a sextant. One of the reasons why knowledge systems within the tribe are limited is the bhagat or the *guru pratha.* In the shamanik system the pupil has to serve the master for a particular period of time. For a tribal to acquire this knowledge, it is imperative for him to be related to the shaman. This is one reason for the limitation of the Banjara knowledge. I can give the example of a shaman. The tribal shaman treats medicines differently. Sometimes medicine is given but at other times there are other systems of dealing with diseases.

The second reason is language. The Gaud-Banjara have a spoken language. It constitutes their self-awareness of their knowledge systems. They do not want their knowledge to go out from their community and be misused, because for them, Knowledge is God. Their entire system of society, family or kinship, is based on the notion of the nayak or shaman. So the spread of their knowledge is possible only if the leader or shaman agrees, otherwise not. The shamans or nayaks are orthodox in their views and they want to preserve the purity of their community. However, the Banjara oral literature acts as a vehicle of transmission of knowledge.

To Ramchandra Guha: Oral communication is a type of communication by itself. A breakdown of communication is caused by aphasia. Looking at tribals in India, do you think there is genuine aphasia among tribals? Or is it that we are not able to understand the way they communicate?

R. Guha: It is not easy to generalise. It is very easy to approach the vulnerable communities and make them feel that they have been attacked. For instance in the Andamans, when the islanders had to face the onslaught of technology, we can say, as Verrier Elwin said in another context, they experienced a 'loss of nerve'. I think among the tribal communities that are more numerous and who are facing economic and political discrimination, the problem is of a different nature.

The tribal communities in Gujarat and Maharashtra have always had to struggle against the non-adivasis. They have a long history of encounter with the political and economic powers. So their culture and language become part of their history of coping and struggling with outsiders. This resistance is also typical to the community. On the other hand, the adivasi community of Australia was in territorial charge of the land. In the eighteenth century the Europeans attacked them, driving them to a geographically marginalised situation in comparison to what it was earlier. When this happened, it can be said that they faced aphasia.

To Subhash Pawra: In Maharashtra there is a community called Pawra. Does their voice reach the society at large? Have they faced conflicts similar to those faced by the Australian adivasi communities?

S. Pawra: In Dhulia district, Pawras do feel the pressure of people around them. I was asked about voicelessness. At one level the leaders are the Pawras themselves. They have representatives in the Government. So their voice does reach a certain level. But at the taluka level, and beyond, there is no communication, though leaders and resource persons from the Pawra community are represented at these levels. However, none of the facilities have ever reached the Pawras in the remote fringes of society. In the district where I live, the Bhil population is more than 50 per cent. They have been able to preserve their *sanskriti.* Where demographically the community is in a minority, it has been in danger of extinction. The same thing can be said about language. Where there are more Pawra Bhils, the Pawra language is preserved. But even in these regions the educated Pawras speak a mixture of Marathi, Hindi and Pawra. The older generation speaks pure Pawra. In the areas where they are in a minority, the purity of the Pawra language has not been preserved. Barring a few Pawra families, it is difficult for most of this community to survive. Very few Pawras have land. Apart from agriculture, they also engage in fishing, collecting forest products or labour. Thus it becomes difficult for them to survive.

To Dhirubhai Patel: If a community loses its resource base, its ability to voice is also curtailed. Both the *bhashas* and forest resources are dwindling in our time. What is the relation of forest and language for the nomadic tribals?

D. Patel: In Dangs, the forest and language are simultaneous. In the beginning, the Forest Department gave a contract to private departments to cut down trees. Before this, the forest was very dense and we used to come across many wild animals. Today even a common bird like a peacock is not seen in the forests though you see many in the urban areas. The moment forests are destroyed the tribals are compelled to scatter, since their life and livelihood are intricately linked with the forest. The Kukna adivasis now have to seek employment in sugar factories elsewhere. They are exposed to standardised Gujarati. Their own language is lost or it starts declining. The Kuknas who have settled in western Gujarat try to imitate sophisticated Gujarati. They cannot express themselves well because the Kukna language forms their subjectivity. They have lost their own language, and have no subjectivity, and so have no real articulation in any other language. The earlier generation used to feel embarrassed about their 'uncivilised' ways. The new generation, however, has embraced the new culture fully.

In 1829, when the British were given the contract to cut trees, they committed atrocities on the tribals in Dangs and harassed the

Kukna tribals. For example, they hanged the tribals and burnt chillies underneath. After independence, funds flowed to the people from the government. But the money never reached the tribals. The money was not used to create an infrastructure. The tribals realised that offering resistance or asking the government for help was useless, that even if they complained, it would be of no use.

To Ajay Dandekar: Is there a relation between depletion of forests and voicelessness?

A. Dandekar: I would say that the knowledge systems of the society are a given. What we need to understand is what this knowledge system was like at one time and how to understand it in today's context. The dominant history of India has by and large ignored the tribals. Various modes of knowledge systems are already there in the tribal tradition. In today's context we have to understand how and from where these systems have emerged. I will speak from the historical perspective. The dominant history says that Indian society, right from the time of the Harappan civilisation, has been primarily an agricultural one. In fact, till the eighteenth century a major part of Indian society had been nomadic. But this fact has been largely ignored and it has been constantly stressed that India is an agricultural society. Even if we consider that communities of people are settled, not nomadic, we should not automatically assume that they are cultivators. Just as historiography has ignored nomadic communities, so in real life too they have been pushed to the periphery. Even sedentary societies that do not preclude agriculture but have some additional subsistence strategies, such as collection of forest and farm produce, are pushed to the margins. It is very easy to state this, but difficult to substantiate historically, because it is difficult to produce evidence to support this theory. It is not that there is no evidence of agriculture, hunting and foodgathering in history. In fact for many centuries, it was the pastoral communities which had been socially, economically and politically dominant and not the societies which were agricultural.

R. Guha: Along with pastoralism and foodgathering, a third mode of subsistence that has been neglected by historiography is shifting agriculture. Only one form of agriculture, i.e. plough agriculture is given prominence.

A. Dandekar: Historians, do not deny the existence of pastoral and foodgathering communities. What they refuse to acknowledge is that these cultures were dominant at one time. Agricultural society means a society doing full-time agriculture like rice agriculture. We do not know if such full-time agriculture existed earlier at a time when these three other sources which were socially, economically and politically dominant. This dominance has to be studied in order to understand the tribal knowledge system.

Jayendra Soni: What you have said of shifting agriculture—is it limited to a particular place or cycle?

A. Dandekar: It depends on what kind of pastoralism is practised. Yes, there is a rhythmic cycle. And the nature of the cycle varies from pastoralism to pastoralism.

To everybody: What is the antonym of aphasia? Can one argue that the English language suffered from 'logorrhoea' due to the diaspora of colonisation, whereas Dangi suffered from aphasia because of the destruction of forests? Can this be said on viewing the status of both the languages today?

To L. Soni: You said that urbanism is creating aphasia. But here everyone seems to hold that when people lose land then there is aphasia. What do you have to say to that?

L.Soni: The case of gypsies in Germany is the same as that of tribals here. It is difficult to apply the concept of aphasia to tribals alone. City people too cannot perceive and articulate themselves properly because of the stressful life. On the other hand the tribals cannot perceive and communicate because of deforestation. I would rather apply aphasia to all civilised parts of society. The question of dominance has to be looked into. And if we regard post-modern society logorrhoea can be seen here too. And this damages communities. In any interaction there are two sides, two groups interacting. Both face a situation of not being able to communicate.

J. Soni: We are dealing with polarities. If we talk of aphasia, we have to talk also of phasia. We cannot get out of the frame of polarities. In order that speech exist and is possible, there also has to be loss of speech. Meaningful speech is associated with meaningless speech.

To R. Guha: Is there a connection between the dwindling of plant species and voicelessness?

R Guha: I would like to speak from the viewpoint of history and the government as well as the government's expectations from the forest and how these state policies affected the society; not from the eyes of the tribals, but as a historian.

In 1829, the British started cutting forests on a large scale. During the nineteenth century, there was large-scale deforestation. One reason was that the rebel princes and their armies used to hide in the forests. So the British cleared the forests. In the 1850s, the British started building railways for transportation of goods and troops.They used to export goods abroad. It was to suppress revolts like 1857 and to build railways that the forests were cut. In 1878, the new forest policy was framed. All the rights of villagers and forest dwellers were taken away. To ensure that there was only a limited population, the land was taken away. It was the first time the State took propriety rights over all kinds of non-cultivable land and wasteland. The villages were asked not to cut trees. This was the first time that such a restriction had been placed. To stem the resistance, one person from each family was allowed to collect fuel, but in very limited quantity. Thus the rights were there, but restricted. There was a lot of resistance to these laws, such as the movements of Birsa Munda in West Bengal and Gudam Ramya in the south. In Bihar the resistance was called the Hul Gulaan. Even on the borders of Orissa and Andhra Pradesh struggles to reclaim the land and the forests for the tribals continued for a long time under the leadership of Aluri Sitaram Raju. We normally tend to lay more emphasis on some points in history and ignore others. The forest *andolans*, forgotten for several years, are being studied now. But even today while Gandhiji and Sardar Patel are recognised as freedom fighters, Birsa Munda, Kalu, Sidhu and the Santhals are ignored. Adivasi leaders in such forest rebellions are largely ignored. Bodos and Mundas also fought valiantly. Yet forest rebellions in tribal communities have not been recorded. We can discover many more such popular rebellions.

L Soni: Were they warrior groups?

R Guha: The Bhils are warriors. And so are the Mundas and the Bodos. Speaking of other communities they are not warriors. These conflicts were inflicted on them and so they turned warriors. The British response to these struggles was to disarm all warrior groups. Those who continued to carry arms were called criminal tribes.

J. Soni: The Zulu tribe carried spears before independence.

R. Guha: In 1947 when we got independence, the communities, hoped that they would get back their land and that they would be allowed to return to the forest. But the forests were given away at almost throwaway prices, almost for free to the new industries coming up.

D. Vadhu: In 1930, both the Salt Law and the Forest Policy were formed. Gandhiji opposed the Salt Law. But the forest laws were not opposed.

Avaneesh Bhatt: In Maharashtra, there were cases of burning tribals in the forests.

To D. Vadhu: 'Civilised' people have always burnt forests and forest dwellers. For instance, the manuscripts of Gunadhya, who composed the *Brihadkatha* in the Paishachik language, were burnt.

The adivasis of Gujarat get 14 per cent reservation in education and employment. The officials may be corrupt but there is corruption even outside the adivasi community. So why don't the adivasis mix with other communities? Do the Dang tribals know there is a '*Bharat Rashtra*'? I know that the Rathwas don't feel so. Their world is limited to Chimnya (Chimanbhai Patel) and Naran (Naransinh Rathwa). Why is there such deliberate ignorance?

D. Vadhu: Of the money set aside for tribal welfare, in the beginning more money was spent on administration. But just constructing school buildings will not lead to education. The education level is very low in tribal areas. There are school buildings, there are funds, the infrastructure is there; but there is no efficient functioning of these schools. There is no sincerity and dedication. For example, in Dangs, teachers decide among themselves to go to the school for one week and to remain absent the next. Seasonal migration for employment is very common. People do not or cannot educate their children. Only some are enlightened and educate their children. Those who stay in the poor areas of the cities, try to educate their children. As a result even within the community rifts appear. One section remains the same as it was fifty years ago and the other section is educated. The communities, which are developed, take advantage of the schemes for tribal welfare. Other backward communities do not know about these schemes. Also, the educated tribal exploits his uneducated brother and thus manipulates the system and his own community. Most families do not know of tribal welfare schemes.

R. Guha: Are the teachers in those schools that you mentioned, tribals?

D. Vadhu: They are a mixed lot.

To S. Pawra: Subhash Pawra is a teacher in a tribal school in a very remote village of Dhulia district. The population is not more than 350. Subhash, why do you miss your teaching sessions though you are a major thinker of the adivasi Pawra community today?

S. Pawra: In most of these areas there is no communication system or transportation available. So it is difficult to commute. If one has to walk, there are the practical difficulties of climbing hills, crossing rivers. One has to travel long distances. The government does not make any proper arrangement for teachers to stay in the village where they are teaching. Even in places where there is an infrastructure, a non-Pawra teacher will not teach because he does not want the Pawra community to progress. I speak from personal experience. In my school, some teachers do not teach because if the Pawra community progresses, it will take advantage of welfare schemes and will be a threat to the community that is at present the dominant community. This has been the practice for many years. Earlier, those who did not go to school, arranged with local leaders to pay money to people to stay away from schools. If only the officers would instead pressurise the teachers to stay in the village and teach, thing would change. But at the moment this is not happening. Earlier, people had wrong notions about education. But today when people want education, the teachers cannot fullfil this responsibility. Political interference has increased. The community is exploited politically. Just to get a single vote, the entire community is manipulated. Teachers who want to teach are harassed. The political leaders are afraid that if the teachers teach, if the community acquires education, the people might become aware of their rights. Those who teach are often harassed, and so they become scared and demotivated. This becomes a major reason for not teaching.

To everybody: Why has there been no Ambedkar among the adivasis? Ambedkar succeeded in transcending the limitations faced by the dalits? So why has no such figure emerged from among the adivasis?

Why do the tribals carry on with their victimhood? Do they want to preserve their sense of being victimised?

S. Pawra: Though the tribals are poor, they live freely and survive independently. If someone like Ambedkar did appear, the inherent unity of this community might decline.

D. Vadhu: Most people in this community just want to earn a livelihood in order to survive. So they do not have time to think of bigger things. Those who are well settled have become indifferent, because they are living in better conditions. I am well settled. I want to articulate issues, but because of this my job gets endangered; mine is a government job. In Jeevan Dhara Yojana, there is a scheme of Rs. 40,000 to help dig wells. On record 1,500 wells have been dug. In actuality, only 150 of these have been dug. Though I am an employee of the bank through which payments were made, I dared not take up this issue. Though these scandals have to be exposed, there is always the fear of political pressure. The schools are there, but teachers are uninterested. In the interior regions the teachers have to work in extremely sordid conditions. The children do not study. Though I feel profoundly disturbed about this, I do not write about these issues. People would come to know that it is I who write, since I am the only person who writes in magazines and newspapers in the Dangs.

A. Dandekar: We have an ancient text called the *Arthashashtra* belonging to the Maurya period. There are long passages in it regarding corruption and punishment. When the British came to India, corruption was already prevalent here. So corruption is not a new phenomenon. That is not really the problem. The problem is that we have a massive land mass inhabited by people with varied customs and varied means of subsistence and varied polities. After seven years of the Kalinga war, Asoka Maurya stated in an inscription that during the Kalinga war many were killed and that he was deeply moved. But even in this remorse he asserted that if the people living in the forests rebelled, he would destroy them. So there were tribal dwellers even in the Maurya period who could defy political power. From the third century B.C. we find an indirect reference that people living in forests and surviving on pastoral medicines were important politically. But the colonial impact was so powerful that from forest-lords they became paupers. Because of the British policies they were forced to move out. Today the psychological impact still persists and so they are not able to cope. The colonial impact has left such a scar, the community feels threatened because of the continued government policies that go against them. This in turn leads to the development of a submissive nature, or on the other hand, to revolts.

A. K. Rathod: The adivasis were affected the most by the changes introduced by the colonisers. The adivasis were thriving once. The destroyed this. Within ten years of the coming of the railways, the Banjaras were declared to be criminals.

To A. K. Rathod: The modern state appears to be the enemy of tradition because the forest policies of the government go against the adivasis. All of us are tied in a social contract. We give tax and the government gives us protection. The adivasi is in contract with nature. The adivasi worships nature. Nature gives him subsistence. Are these two ways of being, these two kinds of contracts conflicting? Do you feel that democracy is being imposed upon the adivasis? Do the adivasis accept the concept of one nation, one constitution?

A. Rathod: This [conflict] is bound to happen. We have to find out where tribal knowledge systems have disappeared, where they have got stuck.

To everybody: Knowledge systems based on logos, are rooted in logic. The adivasi knowledge systems are dominated more by their aesthetics. Modern science and technology are based on the principle of veracity. The adivasi knowledge system is given to students because of their personal loyalty to the shaman and it is nurtured and developed in the same way. Each shaman has a different policy. The modern state has equal laws for all. Our system is based on consensus. But the adivasi tribal system may have different laws for different people. The adivasi community's shaman tradition is personal. Modern technical knowledge is impersonal. Thus the viewpoint of the adivasis towards the state, medicine, law, education, etc. is fundamentally different. So in the light of these polarities, do the adivasis believe in our concept of a united country?

R. Guha: You asked why is there no Ambedkar among the adivasis? I want to know why there has been no successive Ambedkar among the Dalits? Today there is no leader among them like Ambedkar.

To everybody: Ambedkar accepted, thanks to his education in the United States of America, a modern view of life as the ideal way of life and protested against caste politics. Successive generations of dalits interpreted him as a caste politician. Ambedkar got caught in this. He was neither a caste politician nor a political dalit.

J. Soni: Not only in one community but why is there no such figure anywhere else? Why is there no Gandhi elsewhere? There is no person who has made an impact on society as a whole. Each individual fits in a certain context or era. What can be done about this? I, as an individual, should not go beyond my capacity, not only in terms of thinking but also in what I can do. If I in my small way can build the moral calibre of an individual and motivate him to do something in a small way, would it not make a lot of difference? The question as to what I can do is important. We cannot break the framework.

To everybody: Where is the great leader of the adivasis?

A. K. Rathod: The totem system of adivasi exists and they cannot break this. There can be no one single leader among them. They are still deep in their own *sanskriti.* The member of one totem will not believe in another totem.

To A.K. Rathod: Do you respect the god that is worshipped by Subhash Pawra?

A. K. Rathod: Yes, though we worship different gods. If he does not respect mine, I will not respect his.

S. Pawra: In tribal communities they have an indigenous system to manage disputes. As internal justice was meted through internal law, they did not feel the need to approach others.

A. K. Rathod: There is *samuh jeevan* and not *sah jeevan* among adivasis. That is to say, it is 'me against my brother', 'the two of us against our father', 'the three against my family' and 'my family against the clan'.

Avaneesh Bhatt: The dalits are positioned in the fifth place in the *varna-vyavastha*. Adivasis have no place here. But, at one time, there was tremendous mobility within this social structure. So it was not fixed.

R. Guha: In the caste system there used to be internal mobility. For example, a shudra could become a Rajput but not so an adivasi.

To Rajendra Nanavati: Why is the knowledge of adivasis not known to us? The tradition of tribal knowledge is oral. In Sanskrit there was a storehouse of knowledge. Most of it was oral. Some of it was written. How did Sanskrit continue to develop despite this through oral means? Why did so many branches of knowledge develop in Sanskrit? In the Sanskrit tradition a third century thinker like Bharata was known to a tenth century thinker like Abhinavagupta, who would then continue his predecessor's tradition. At the folk level, stories from *Ramayan*, were remembered and people went on adding to this.Why?

R. Nanavati: Actually, the *guru-shishya parampara* has been a cconstant feature in Sanskrit literature and there has been a give and take. For example, in the sixth century, both Bhamaha and Dandin flourished in Sanskrit literature by reading each other's works. This is a continuous process and by correcting the mistakes made by the earlier writer the successors developed their own knowledge stock. If Bhamaha criticises a poem saying that it is not a poem, Dandin on the other hand calls it *swabhava-vrutti.* Anandavardhan corrects the mistakes of Vaman. For more than one thousand years, right from Bharata to Jagannath, the tradition has been continuous. There was no break in between

To everybody: In the *guru-shishya parampara,* the adivasis' knowledge has been slow in its growth. In the context of adivasi knowledge would you agree or disagree with Dr. Nanavati's statement?

D. Vadhu: In ethnomedicine there are certain formulae, which are secret and are not transmitted. Because of this tradition where the formulae are secret, it is possible that further growth of knowledge does not take place and knowledge is handed down only on a limited scale. There are chances of knowledge remaining stagnant.

To everybody: What are the methodologies of learning *mantra-vidya?* Do you think that because of this methodology the adivasi tradition of *mantra-vidya* or chant has not been developed?

Subhash Ishai: There are two ways of learning *mantras.* One is the familiar tradition where the badvo [shaman] father may teach the son. The *mantras* do not remain in the exact original form when the father recites the *mantras* and the son learns them. It is not only that he may make his own additions, but also that his *mantras* may differ from his father's. In the second tradition it is the divinities that teach the *mantra.* This is not very common.

To Kocharbhai, the Shaman: Kocharbhai, you know *mantra-vidya?* You are a very important shaman in this area. Do you plan to transmit your knowledge to anyone else? And how will you do this?
Kocharbhai Rathwa: I will not teach *mantras* to my son. My son

will get them in a dream. God will inspire him to learn them. I learnt them on my own. It is nature's gift through the divine.

Shankarbhai Rathwa: I do not chant the *mantras* automatically. I have to learn them.

Kocharbhai: Nobody can teach *mantras*. If somebody teaches *mantras*, they are not *mantras* any longer.

Shankarbhai: You know *mantras*? Who taught you the *mantras*?

Kocharbhai: Automatic!

Subhash Ishai: When you learnt the *mantras* you must have practised or experienced something?

Kocharbhai: I do not remember.

Subhash Ishai: Did you observe *punam*?[1]

Kocharbhai: Occasionally.

Subhash Ishai: Did you fast?

Kocharbhai: At times.

Subhash Ishai: What else did you do?

Kocharbhai: Nothing.

To Mansingh Rathwa: Mansinghbhai, where did you learn the art of *pithora* painting? It is a record of oral history.

---

[1] Fasts and austenties observed at the full moon.

Mansingh: My ancestors used to paint in the King's palace. The tradition was handed down from father to son and so I learnt it.

To Mansingh Rathwa: Do you paint pithoras as your father did or in a different manner?

Mansingh: We basically paint as my ancestors did. Now we have improved upon it. Now we have added new things like images of television, vehicles, etc.

S. Pawra: The pithora is a procession of a wedding. Now they have seen television, trains and cars. And so they are adding these.

R. Guha: Is there any change in the methodology? Why do you paint pithoras?

Mansingh: Out of interest.

To Mansingh Rathwa: Do you spend time teaching it to others?

Mansingh: I enjoy teaching it to others. I teach anyone who is interested—young people, my children, everyone.

To Mansingh Rathwa: Do you know the story behind the pithora painting?

Mansingh: We know painting and the tradition. I do not know the entire story of pithora. Only badvas can tell this.

To Kocharbhai: Kocharbhai, do you know the story of pithora?

Kocharbhai : Yes, but I cannot tell it now. It is sacred.

Mansingh: The story of pithora is a poem. It should be recited only at the time of a ritual. Not at other times.

To everyone: Mohanbhai is a weaver. Where did you learn this art?

Mohanbhai: From my parents.

To Mohanbhai: Will you teach it to someone?

Mohanbhai: Yes, to my sons.

To Mohanbhai: Do you sing songs while weaving?

Mohanbhai: No.

To Mohanbhai: Are there any religious ceremonies or *mantras* to be observed?

Mohanbhai: We recite *mantras* at the time of beginning the work. We recite the Saraswati *mantra* and light a *diya* because Saraswati gave us knowledge. By this the work acquires purity.

A. K. Rathod: Banjaras also pray in the same manner.

To Kocharbhai Varia: Kodarbhai, you make beautiful pottery. Where did you learn this art? Whom will you transmit it to? Do you believe that this is a *vidya?*

Kocharbhai: When Lord Shankar called all the kings of the universe then Lord Shankar made a golden throne for all the potters. Many great kings came and we kept on receding in the backdrop. When Lord Shankar appeared in the assembly he first called us. As we were seated at the back, we replied to him from there. He told us that he had made the throne for us so that we would be able to sit in the front. Then he cursed us that as we were seated at the back we would always be heard last. In every occasion - at marriages, at deaths, etc. we would always be heard last. Even today this practice continues.

To Chamulal Rathwa: Chamubhai, the adivasis traditionally learn through oral exchange. Students keep on adding new things to the existing fund of knowledge. Is it possible that because of the practice of oral tradition, adivasi children are unable to learn in modern schools?

C. Rathwa: First, I will speak of the magical chants. My father liked me a lot and I had a lot of curiosity. I wanted to learn *mantras* from him but he did not teach me. I asked him why he did not teach me the *mantras*. I told him that I believed in *mantras* and had witnessed their powers. Despite my faith he did not teach me. I used to roam the forests with my father. Once when I accompanied him to the jungle, we came across a tiger. My father recited a *mantra*, raised his hand and the tiger stopped short. This way I have personally experienced the power of *mantras*.

To Kocharbhai: Kocharbhai, can you do the same?

Kocharbhai: No.

Shankarbhai Tadvi: What one can do, another cannot. It is a matter of faith.

C. Rathwa: When I asked my father he said that it is like operating a machine. And it functions only in a particular way. As you require skills to operate a machine, you have to acquire certain skills and particular norms of behaviour to learn chants. Just as when the skill is not properly acquired the machine may become ineffective, so if the norms are not acquired properly, the chants may go against one. You need a rare kind of confidence and personal discipline. You have to observe certain norms. The present generation is not capable of acquiring the norms and so not capable of learning the chants. Because of the fear that the next generation will not observe the norms properly, my generation did not pass on the knowledge and so my generation has lost this knowledge.

R. Guha: Just as your father had knowledge, which you don't have, is it possible that you have some knowledge that the earlier generation did not have ?

C. Rathwa: Yes, there is some knowledge of *vanaspati*, like certain herbs, their origins and use, of which I learnt later. I now realise that I should have talked of this to my father. Later, I asked someone about this but he did not give me the information either. It is kept secret.

S. Pawra: There are bhagats. Each bhagat may have four to five children. In the family the eldest or youngest son are traditionally offered the *maan* or authority to perform the duty of bhagat. They hold a special position. According to tradition they have the right to carry forward the tradition of bhagat. At the time of worship society pays them special honour. Even if they do not have the capability to inherit the tradition, they can observe their father doing these duties and so carry on the tradition. The performance of the son may go wrong. But the community marks these mistakes and corrects him. And so the son hones his skill in performing duties. He learns the chants and tries to imbibe them properly. He may make mistakes initially. There are different types of rituals, which have to be observed while reciting the chants. For example, a badva may recite a mantra to make a person get well while a pujara may merely worship. He might not be able to heal a sick person.

To everybody: Are pujaras and badvas different?

D. Vadhu: Among us, in the Dangs the same person plays the roles of badva and pujara, he is called the bhagat.

To everybody: If we speak of all communities, then among the Pawras, the badva (shaman) and pujara (priest), among the Dehwalis the pujaras (who performs the marriage and other religious ceremonies) and bhagat (who can treat people and knows magical chants), among the Banjaras the bhagat (who holds more power) and maharaja (who can perform simple rites) are traditionally found.

S. Pawra: Among them we also find singers at times who sing both popular and religious songs. They know the stories related to the gods. Sometimes at the time of religious ceremonies, these singers are specially invited to sing.

C. Rathwa: According to Subhash Pawra, it is the bhagat's son who inherits his tradition. My father taught my brother and me differently according to our capabilities. What my brother learnt was not taught to me and vice versa.

A. K. Rathod: The elder son has the right to learn, or according to Chamulal one is taught according to one's capability. This tradition has existed since the time of the *Ramayana*. In the *Ramayana* it was the elder son of Dashrath who got the throne. This tradition, begun by Valmiki, continues even today.

S. Pawra: These days, an educated person's education is only towards western, scientific knowledge. Uneducated persons alone are interested in acquiring this system of knowledge after their day's work is over. Educated persons deprive themselves of this knowledge.

A. Dandekar: There is no standardised text of *Ramayana*. There are 463[1] versions of *Ramayana*. There is no label of authenticity attached to any of these texts. So we should be aware of which *Ramayana* is being discussed.

G. N. Devy: The Oriental Institute has published a critical text on the *Ramayana*.

R. Nanavati: But that is based only on Valmiki's *Ramayana*.

---

[1] The figure needs to be verified. However it is true that numerous 'folk' *Ramayanas* are in circulation in India.

To everybody: So, going by your response, may I say that among the adivasis there are four modes of getting knowledge:

1. *Kala*: Anyone can learn and teach an art like the painting of pithora.
2. Sacred knowledge: This is confined to a few persons and can be learnt only by a few persons, for example, *mantra vidya*.
3. Traditional science: That includes medicine, scientific knowledge, construction of houses, preserving seeds, and is available to all.
4. Medicinal knowledge: This is sometimes secret and at times it is accessible to everyone.

The community passes on traditional knowledge from one generation to the next. Sacred knowledge is personal in nature, and an individual passes this secretly to another. The present forms of imparting knowledge in schools and colleges are different. These institutions do not recognise the traditional forms of tribal knowledge as valid. Therefore, today we should not ask whether the adivasi has any forms of knowledge, perhaps instead we should ask what is knowledge? Can we say only what the formal institutions teach be termed as knowledge, or can we say that what the adivasis possess is also knowledge? The central question is what is knowledge?

R. Guha: This is a very difficult question.

R. Nanavati: One has to establish adivasi knowledge as 'Knowledge'. How do you establish the validity of this knowledge? Their knowledge is effective, I accept, but it is for us to take this knowledge, put this knowledge in a broader perspective and recognise it. For example, if a particular medicine can cure a certain illness then who will recognise this as knowledge in society? It is for us to resolve this.

S. Pawra: Tribal knowledge is not recognised in society because of certain beliefs of the people. Established forms of knowledge in particular surround the modern world at large as well as the adivasi communities. It is believed by society that tribal knowledge is based on superstition. They would ask us to go to hospitals. Who would accept our knowledge of medicine?

A. Dandekar: Dominance of knowledge is associated with power. What is knowledge and what is not knowledge is decided in the context of power. Those who have power in society believe that only what they possess is knowledge and as the adivasis do not have political power, what knowledge they have is not recognised as such.

R. Nanavati: There is the question of knowledge, and particularly the knowledge that is useful and to which we still have to give scientific validity. We can establish facts in a laboratory. But the adivasis do not have such means. Who will give validity and respectability to the vast store of adivasi knowledge? It is a question of processing knowledge in acceptable formats. It is to be established that this knowledge *is* knowledge.

A.K. Rathod: The society perhaps will not go against accepting medicine but against the rituals associated with acquiring knowledge, for instance that of worshipping trees before collecting the produce. In Maharashtra there is an area of Gond adivasis, Purkheli village, where a super-specialist medical scientist is doing research on adivasi medicine. He has also published a book on this.

A. Dandekar: This is an example of the exception proving the rule. In India, wherever there are now dams and major irrigation facilities, those were once adivasi areas. So actually adivasis and their knowledge have, more often than not, been totally ignored. Only empowerment can recognise knowledge. In the Constitutional Amendment of 1996, it is stated that to extract products from any adivasi designated area, one has to get the approval and consent of the people of that area.

To Nagin Rathwa: Nagin, you study in a college. Do you learn any positive things about adivasis there? Do you believe that your education will help you in life?

Nagin Rathwa: In college we get deep knowledge about various subjects.

To N. Rathwa: Have you received any deep knowledge about life?

Nagin Rathwa: No, this has not been the case.

To N. Rathwai: Is there any future for any little knowledge the adivasis have?

C. Rathwa: There are two categories of knowledge:

1. That which deals with the metaphysical, such as chants, etc.
2. That which deals with practical aspects, for example, how to live, how to catch fish etc.

Practical knowledge is learnt with your own eyes only, while metaphysical knowledge is acquired through the mind. So its future is not sure. To get metaphysical knowledge one has to devote oneself completely to its pursuit, which is not possible today. So this metaphysical knowledge is threatened. There is a fundamental difference between what children learn in schools and the practical knowledge which they receive at home. Children easily grasp what they learn at home and in their surroundings. They find it difficult to learn at school.

It is said that many arts like fishing are being lost. Why should a person not spend Rs. 30 and buy fish rather than go fishing and lose out on a job of Rs. 200. Each issue should be thought through differently. One cannot earn enough money by following the traditional tribal systems. And with every import of a new occupation and technology the traditional knowledge is threatened.

R. Nanavati: There are certain adivasi branches of knowledge like medicine and astronomy, which have been acquired through observation, for example, forecasting weather. These observations refer to the cycle of nature and should be preserved.

Shankarbhai: I have a different view. Whatever knowledge the adivasis have must be preserved.

To the Reader: We can learn a lot from the adivasi way of *nirikshan* or observation power that forms the essence of the adivasi knowledge system. We need to understand not merely *what* is known (the content of knowledge) but *how* one gets to know what one knows (the process of acquiring and transmitting. knowledge). This mode of getting knowledge, if known to the larger society, will help transform the education system. This is what the rest of the world has to learn from the adivasis. The question is, will it ?

7

Development*

I

Years ago when I first started working in adivasi areas, the term 'development' frequently cropped up in the social discourse I had to encounter. Whenever I was being introduced to strangers, my friends would say 'Professor Devy has been working on the issue of adivasi development'. I however, was not sure as to what exactly was meant by development. While discussing various government progammes and their implementation I used to hear expressions such as 'beneficial to adivasi development', and 'in the interest of adivasis'. But it was not clear what exactly development meant.

Upon asking my adivasi friends, 'What exactly does development mean to you?' their response generally was 'We need roads in such and such a place', or 'This village needs a school'. But one adivasi friend stated that it would be nice to have more mahua trees. His response compelled me to think more carefully on the subject of 'development'.

In the initial years of my work with the adivasis, I had many opportunities of participating in seminars and conferences about adivasi development. A lot was discussed at these events and a multitude of approaches were advocated. But in these discussions adivasis were usually quantified in terms of 'thousands' and 'millions' instead of being characterised as 'adivasis gathering mahua flowers' as against 'adivasis working in cities as labourers'. I also heard in very structured terms how this or that Commissioner for Tribal

Development had issued a variety of circulars and office orders to his staff. But my basic question as to what development really is, remained unanswered in these forums. Perhaps, this was because of my own intellectual inadequacy.

Subsequently, the Adivasi Academy was founded at Tejgadh and a post graduate diploma programme was established. The first batch of the diploma programme attracted fifteen students of whom thirteen were adivasis. There was no clear roadmap of what would be taught in this programme of instruction. All my student friends had completed three years of studies in a college. But I do not think that any of them had read books written by any acclaimed Gujarati authors. Neither were they aware of the existence of different states and regions in India. And it would be best not to comment on their familiarity with the English language.

Initially, I had thought that everyone in this group would first learn to operate computers, then start reading books in English, Gujarati and Hindi, and would in general become aware of the modern world like students elsewhere. I tried hard to accomplish these goals during the first few months of our work together. But instead of seeing a change in the approach of the students, I noticed that my own ideas and thoughts on the subject of education had started undergoing a change. First of all I realised that the assumption about the validity of certain thought processes which I had come to accept for my intellectual transactions over the decades had to be radically questioned. I realised that my own views on history, society, culture and politics had to be set aside and an attempt had to be made to see the world through the eyes of my students. Instead of changing the thinking of fifteen individuals, I thought, it would be better for me to make those individuals my teachers and to begin exploring every aspect of life according to their world-vision. So I did away with the course-work and started an open-ended dialogue with them on life, learning and development.

During the initial phase of the Adivasi Academy, the Tejgadh panchayat had rented a small room to us for use. We used it to store office files, library books and other materials. For our discussions we used an open plot at Mandar. Mandar is the area in Tejgadh where the campus of the Academy is now situated. This plot had been given to us by the government to build the Academy's campus, but so far no building had been constructed. When the sun got scorching hot, we would move to the shade of the giant mahua tree. Under the shade of the mahua's lush branches during the heat of the day, and in the evenings, on open craggy rocks, our discussions would continue from noon to evening, and often through the night.

During these discussions, I realised that these students possessed an intelligence of a different kind. They had clear views on every issue. They articulated their opinions very lucidly. They did not rely on jargon or cliches to prove a point. They did not imitate anyone.

My student friends had to leave their homes early in the morning after eating a meal of *rotla* or maize bread. They would stay with me throughout the day without having lunch. In the first few months, a person from Tejgadh used to bring lunch for me cooked by a family in Tejgadh. As I ate my lunch, the students would read files, books and newspapers in the library. Some chewed tobacco or smoked. After a while it occurred to me that it was not right for me to have lunch when the students remained hungry. So I changed the routine a little. I decided that first of all if discussions stretched into the lunch hour, I would forgo lunch. And if it became impossible for me to control my hunger, the time of the discussions would have to be changed. The question of hunger started occupying my thoughts during my daily commute between Tejgadh and Vadodara.

After our group had completed a year of study, we received the news that some starving adivasis in Chattisgarh, had, in an attempt to stave off the pangs of hunger, eaten a dead pig, and had subsequently died of food poisoning. This incident occurred on 15 August 2001. The death by starvation of adivasis fifty-five years after independence would have shocked me even when I was a university teacher. But now, because I had seen the hunger of my student friends from very close quarters, this incident made a deep impression on me. I decided to give up one meal a day. I wrote a letter to the Prime Minister asking that village food banks be established to prevent adivasis and other vulnerable sections of

Indians from dying of malnutrition and hunger. Subsequently, along with Smt Mahasweta Devi, Shri Laxman Gaikwad and Dr Ajay Dandekar, I met the Prime Minister in Delhi, on 12 september 2001. The meeting was arranged by Shri George Fernandes. Some weeks later the government announced its decision to establish foodgrain banks in 1,16,000 villages. After the announcement I once again resumed eating two meals a day.

The students' lack of interest in reading academic books, or in imitating urban lifestyles, and their clarity of thought — all these characteristics and habits were rooted in the context of their experience of hunger. I felt that people touched by hunger, whether in India or in other countries, would have similar views. Perhaps they have firm convictions about what is appropriate for human beings and what is not. Their convictions and views deserve to be understood and articulated. The desire to do so took firm hold of my mind. I began to think afresh about development.

II

The modern discourse on development has come to India from the west. It has evolved over three to four centuries in specific historical and social contexts. This concept is dominated by the widely prevalent technological and industrial culture. Nature's law of 'survival of the fittest' forms the ideological framework of that discourse. Development in that ideology means digging up the earth, turning it over, exploring it and formulating new products, metals and chemicals. It admits of wars to procure unrestricted rights on those resources. It means collecting innumerable weapons to fight these wars; allows commanding these wars, spreading this ideology everywhere by strengthening the state's power of coercion through supporting legal structures. It means feeding into the greed of human beings by institutionalising greed! This discourse of development has been globally accepted. Thanks to the prevailing developmental discourse, terms like 'privatisation', 'democracy', 'globalisation', and 'progress' have acquired global legitimacy.

Even those opposing social structures and economies based

upon the principle of 'limitless greed' are unable to come up with an alternate definition of development. They ask, 'Privatisation is definitely an important idea, but isn't it also important to simultaneously have limits on greed and the profit motive?' 'Law and order have to be obeyed, but isn't it equally important to oppose the violence and genocide that come along with it?' 'It is important that everyone become literate, but should we give so much importance to the written script in our communications?' These questions are raised from a combination of certain ethical and pragmatic concerns. When such ethical questions arise, it is usually noticed that the people who ask these questions have pre-formulated notions. They do not want to accept changes in social transactions because their interests lie in maintaining a status quo. To idealise 'development' and support it for furthering personal interests, as well as to oppose the concept of development to protect personal interests, are two sides of the same coin. The real issue of development has got lost between these seemingly important considerations of ethics and economics. As far as ethics are concerned, we know that they are not based on any perennially valid principles. Ethics change in every age. Therefore, one cannot say that a given set of ethical norms has perennial validity.

Nor can development be seen only as linked to economic considerations. Improvement of the quality of life does not hinge entirely on economic betterment.

Rather than thinking of development in terms of ethics or economics we might think of it in other ways. Development is a profoundly political and cultural concern. Political, because the conceptualisation of the distinction between development and backwardness rests on political considerations. Cultural, because every village, every country needs its own unique idea of development. In that sense to have a global definition or a common global norm for development does not make sense.

Social development and political transactions are profoundly interlinked. The cultural impact of development has tremendous lasting power.

III

My student friends from the Tejgadh Academy defined development according to what seemed appropriate to their own context. According to their understanding, development implies creating villages where starvation and deprivation do not force people to migrate out of the village, where no one dies of malnutrition, where no one becomes a bonded labourer under the burden of debt, where no one is exploited because he/she is illiterate, and where every patient has some access to medical facilities. When this definition found a verbal articulation in the group, everyone's faces lit up as though they had just seen a pleasant dream. Indeed this notion of development is the dream of the poor who are trying to survive in the seven hundred thousand villages of India.

It is sad that so many years after independence, India's rural masses, and to some extent the poor in the cities too, remain deprived of drinking water, primary education and primary healthcare. The boundaries of the cities are rapidly expanding to include the villages situated close to them. These villages are getting caught in the horror of transformation into city slums. As small villages become big they start imitating the cities. But in the end they continue to exist as underprivileged small towns. The quality of education in their schools and colleges is substandard. The quality of health care is poor. In the midst of dirt, sickness and unemployment they wait in vain for development to come their way.

The first thing that strikes a visitor to any of India's big cities is the stench in the air. Travelling outside the metropolis, the imaginary visitor comes across uncultivated land stretching on both sides of the railway tracks for hundreds of kilometres. Arriving in any small town, he realises that these so-called small towns have an alarming density of population. Every place is infested with mosquitoes, and the electricity supply is extremely unreliable. The railway stations are enveloped in stench and show the sorry sight of helpless people gathered there in search of a temporary shelter. When the imaginary traveller continues his journey he arrives in the countryside where villages are overflowing with poorly planned concrete houses built in imitation of city-dwellings, where open gutters flow near the vegetable vendors' carts and grocery stores, and where mosquitoes breed in the puddles and potholes on the roads. When he goes still further he sees tiny villages, linked by narrow dirt roads but which look favourably upon agricultural activity. Upon looking at the villager's clothes, faces and houses our imaginary traveller may be led to think that these villages have recently experienced a major natural disaster. This travelogue of our imaginary traveller is quite unsettling; but is it far from the truth about our country?

Some may argue that this picture is superficial and biased. Why doesn't this hypothetical traveller focus on the progress we have made? There is some substance to this argument. Side by side with the squalour and poverty, our country is experiencing the rapid advent of a strange economic revolution. Its imprint can be seen on the billboards in every city. The signboards on the broken buses of our State Transportation Corporation suggest to us the great deeds accomplished by the government. The clubs and air-conditioned convention centres in cities like Mumbai, Delhi and Ahmedabad give us a taste of this revolution. The credit cards that are widely circulated by most banks bear the signature of this revolution. The English language newspapers printed on pink paper, focusing on economic issues, emit the fragrance of this revolution. The cars, refrigerators and changing tones of the cell phones used by the upper middle class fill our ears with the music of this revolution. The magical insignia of an American visa in a person's passport as life's most precious achievement is the sole obsession of the class benefited by the new revolution. Can this be an economic revolution? Can this at all be our ultimate claim to development?

When my adivasi friends created their definition of development, I saw in their eyes, just once or twice, a question mark. The question was 'Is it likely that we will stand the risk of missing out on the economic revolution happening elsewhere if we take up the cause of this newly defined development? What if we never get an opportunity to satisfy our desire for economic wellbeing through the new economic revolution?'

My students and I continued our discussions, thinking and work. There were moments when I feared that perhaps under my influence they were concealing their natural instinct of material greed. I even feared for a while that the communication between them and me would snap because of the 'unnaturalness of the ideas' in our experiment. At times I wondered if I was forcing them on a path that they had not wanted to take, or else, whether they would suddenly turn away from this new and meaningful definition of rural development, which they had conceptualised themselves. But at the same time when I saw their enthusiasm in discussion and action, I felt reassured that these were extremely creative and committed activists. They were enlightened from within. The world's greatest temptations could not influence them. I became convinced that I was not their teacher; rather they were, collectively, my guide.

After a lot of thought, I decided to put down on paper all the ideas that had come up in our discussion during these two years of life and work together. When there is a storm raging all around, how long can a small candle continue to provide light? If I write down all the thoughts developed at the Tejgadh Academy, then maybe they will inspire someone else to do some other work with adivasis.

At this juncture I feel it appropriate to say something about my adivasi student friends with whom I have mapped new ideas of development. It may be necessary to understand the circumstances in which the creators of these ideas live in order to appreciate the gravity of their ideas.

Naginbhai Rathwa, Narayanbhai Rathwa, and Govindbhai Rathwa are residents of Tejgadh's Hardaspur quarters. Naginbhai and Narayanbhai are not even twenty-five years old and Govindbhai is perhaps four or five years older. All three have B.A. degrees. All three of them have the ability to organise major events with very little outside help. They are all taciturn. A peculiar adivasi intellect glimmers in their eyes. Naginbhai had once wished to renounce everything and become a sanyasi. Now he is anxious to work for the benefit of adivasi society; but he wants to stay away from politics. He stands tall and has a very expressive smile. Narayanbhai has a poet's sensibility. He is interested in literature and literary activities, and believes in doing everything in a disciplined manner. Govindbhai is simple as a saint in everything. He is always happy as though there is an unending source of music within him. He reminds me of Narsi Mehta.

Shaklabhai, Vireshbhai, and Gumanbhai Rathwa are from the Panwad area. Shaklabhai's village is Shihada which is close to Panwad. He is very cheerful. Like a trainee soldier, his excitement in things new is tempered by self-control. He is very perceptive and is perennially willing to volunteer for good work. Vireshbhai is comparatively gentler. His eyes seem to be eternally questioning modernity. He is always lost in thought, always tormented by ethical dilemmas. He is very knowledgeable about adivasi cultural history, but at the same time he is also preoccupied with the deprivation that has come as a result of this cultural past. At a very young age, Gumanbhai came in contact with Christian culture because of which his style of posing questions is very different from that of the others. He is a committed volunteer. But because of economic difficulties he is always under mental stress, which sometimes makes him very edgy. He is extremely generous and, like Govindbhai, never gets angry.

There is another Naginbhai. To differentiate him from the Naginbhai from Hardaspur, we refer to him as Naginbhai C. Rathwa. Naginbhai Rathwa is older, and as a result, more experienced. His manner of working is extremely disciplined and flawless. Had he been in Mumbai he would have been an administrator in some corporation. Naginbhai Rathwa would perhaps never have a pending file on his table.

Hemsinghbhai Rathwa is probably the same age as Naginbhai C. Rathwa and exhibits an extraordinary political awareness. His eyes are always red. I had earlier assumed that due to his habit of brooding he is unable to sleep soundly. Later I realised that he suffers from an eye disease. I imagine Hemsinghbhai some years from now: He is pouring over books until late at night under a solar lamp, bespectacled and worried about how to create a just and fair society; his checked shirt is ruffled by the slow breeze.

Manharbhai Rathwa strives hard in very unfavourable conditions to help his village of Moti-Amrol become self-reliant. He has a good awareness of the changes taking place in the political and cultural climate. He fights for the rights of adivasis. The glimmer in his eyes reminds one of the glint of the arrows used by his ancestors.

Rajendrabhai Variya is ever ready to spread happiness though his own life is beset with difficulties. When he works to set up a health-camp one gets the impression that a European doctor has come to serve the villages. The dominant characteristic in Rajendrabhai's nature is the spirit of service. Whenever a feeling of pride surfaces in him, he readily turns towards serving people as a curative measure. He is very resourceful and trustworthy.

Vasantbhai Rathwa is a resident of Tejgadh. He is highly intelligent and at the same time has the gift of articulating his observations logically. He is not easily influenced by anyone. He arrives at his own conclusions and has the patience to implement his decisions. He likes to look at modernity with an open mind. He wants to give adivasi children a good education.

Manishabhen Variya is also from Tejgadh. Had she lived in a city she would have become a lecturer in a college. She has an M.A. degree. In the last three or four years she has organised women's savings groups and has been able to creat the seemingly impossible saving of one and half million rupees. She is a shining example of what a committed woman can do towards the benefit of society.

Shailesh Patel came to Tejgadh from Panchmahal's Kothamba area. He has a charismatic personality. He believes it is his duty to do good work. He is a great organiser and a good speaker. Sometimes he gets emotional on seeing the sorrows of others.

Kantibhai Vasava is from the Narmada district. He wants to progress in a career in the teaching field. He has good knowledge of history and political systems. All these students were my teachers.

IV

What follows is a document based on the ideas that we as a group have thought through in our work together at the Adivasi Academy at Tejgadh.

Development is a ceaseless process. Families and the society decide new benchmarks at every stage of development; only if we work towards these goals can there be continuous development. The nature of a river is to keep flowing; the same is true of development. The beginning of development comes from the definite urge for bringing about a change in a person, family and the society. If people do not have the desire to bring about this change, how will development take place? The beginning of development is in the mind of an individual.

To bring about development doesn't mean to acquire more consumer goods or to gain more wealth. Development means to become free and fearless.

True development is that which comes from within. That which comes from outside is called aid. The strength of a person who becomes dependent on outside help goes on diminishing; with only outside help how can development happen? Only that development which comes from within and uplifts the human being and society is the true development.

There is a very old rule of the world: Things change, they keep changing continuously. In some countries, society changes very fast. In comparison to them, if one's speed of change is slower then all will say 'you are not developed', 'you are backward'? But what is backwardness? Who decides that a certain society is backward?

No person, society or country is backward from the beginning. When a society or a person stops thinking about development and prefers to stay like a herd of sheep then the speed of development decreases and backwardness creeps in. Also the more powerful countries consider the countries which are economically less prosperous as backward. But such an appellation in fact only serves to make it possible to exploit such a 'backward country'. Truly speaking, backwardness is not the given condition of a society. It is not a proper description of any society. It is a perception resulting from the need for economic competition. Though development is seen as a specific condition of a society and is a term used to describe a society, it should never contain a sense of the hierarchical ranking of societies, nor should it stem from a situation of economic competitiveness and a feeling of comparison.

What is development? How to bring about development? Who will create it? From where do we begin this process of development? The feeling of comparison should have no role to play in any thinking about development, because an activity which may be good for one village may not be development for some other village. In fact, it can become the cause of its destruction. Every river flows; but have you ever seen two rivers flow alike?

Development does not happen by imitating others. By imitating villages, the cities will not develop; and by imitating cities, the villages cannot develop. The nature of villages is of one kind and that of the cities is of a different kind. The villages in our ancestor's times were good, full of forests and water. The cattle used to get good fodder in those days. Human beings used to get proper meals and a place to stay. There were no quarrels over natural resources. There was harmony and respect. In every adivasi village one could hear songs and see dances. The people who composed these songs and dances before us were living in such bliss!

Who created such beautiful villages? With what means? With what intentions? What is it that the people then had that we do not have?

Did they have more farming land? Did they have more money? Were they more intelligent than we are? More and 'less' – these words, though often used in connection with the idea of development, have absolutely no connection with it. We have schools, hospitals, and means of transportation, fertilisers to spray in farms, newspapers, radios, and new laws to fight the caste system. Yet we are not 'developed' nor are we happy. 'More' and 'less' – these words do not have any relation to development.

It is not true that hunger gives rise to sadness or that wealth produces happiness. Greed is the cause of unhappiness, and happiness comes from the feeling of fulfilling our duty. The bread which we make today is the same bread that our ancestors used to eat. Then how is it that they were so happy and we are not? The reason is that greed has become legitimised now. Everywhere in this world an atmosphere of increasing greed has developed. The habit of acquiring more and more of everything is spreading in all directions. There is a growing trend to acquire things we do not need. Our ancestors knew what was necessary and what was not. We have lost that quality. Our ancestors were happier than us not because they had 'more' of any *thing,* but because of their good sense. Development means cultivating that good sense.

Comparison with one another, and competition with other societies and countries have only increased our greed. Not just to accumulate capital, but to maintain and increase it unlimitedly is what the 'developed' societies consider production. In their eyes the greed for more means production. Not to have such greed means that a society has not progressed. But rather than 'developed' would it not be more appropriate to simply call such people greedy?

To satisfy our greed, more and more things have to be manufactured. To do the work of humans, machines have to be built. The value of a human being has become even less than that of a machine. A human being is what we get easily by paying money for labour, as if one were some slow-moving machine bought to be exploited.

To sell these manufactured goods, new markets have to be created. We have to market and advertise those products. In these advertisements there is no need to be too particular about what is truth and what is fiction. As long as the product sells, the advertisers' purpose is fulfilled. Are such people 'developed' who keep other human beings like animals, who hoard food, even when not hungry, who have greed for far more things than they will ever need, who have no respect for familial and social ties? Are they sensible or vicious? Viciousness is not development. Sensibility is development.

Countries with unlimited greed create new markets by making other countries their slaves; they cripple humanity. This is not just greed but an act of violence. These countries create fights among various nations, and in these wars they sell arms and ammunitions to the misled quarrellers. Are such war-mongers developed? Who is going to develop by this? By this, only war, violence and riots will increase. Should we call such people developed or should we call them destructive?

Food is needed to satisfy hunger. In spite of having enough food and foodgrains in the country as well as in the world, nearly thirty per cent of our population is underfed, and people are hungry. Is this development or destruction? The world is gripped by the global politics of hunger. On one side there are mountains of grains and food while on the other side there are rivers of tears from starving people. Is this development or destruction? Is this progress or regress?

In their unlimited greed they exploit nature in every way and in every place. Birds suffocate in the polluted air; fish burn in the polluted waters. Trees are alienated from their roots and the earth is destroyed by poisonous fertilisers. But the greed of 'developed' people shows no sign of diminishing. Are such people civilised? How can development happen without fresh air and clear water, healthy roots and peaceful minds? And development of what? Does this pollution mean development for mankind or death for nature?

We have heard that education brings about development. This is true. But where there is poverty of thought, where children do not learn anything but get tired due to the burden of books and tension from exams, where childhood is lost altogether in the anxiety of securing one's adulthood, can this be called education? Is there any room for knowledge where people earn their degree certificates by cheating? That education which is finally of no use, which has no connection with practical life, what kind of education is that? Does such education lead to development or wipe away whatever intelligence is left?

We see that in the desire for development, our youth have started going towards the city. We know how little they are respected there. The young men and women who leave for the cities stay there till they become old. They forget their roots, they lose themselves and they begin to think that this madness is 'development' What should we say to them; what can we learn from them?

V

There was a village.

The air there was not polluted.

The water there was not polluted.

The farmers used natural manure, and the fields yielded rich crops.

The young people stayed on in the village and did not hanker to go to cities. They said, 'Why should we imitate city life? Why don't we make our village like the city so that we don't have to migrate?'

The farmers living in the village were surprised. They said, 'Children, why do you harbour such foolish thoughts? Times have changed. It is essential for you to go to the city. How else can your sons and daughters go to America and England? Forget this *dhoti* and *kurta*. Drop your bow and arrow. Do not touch the plough. Wear trousers and T-shirts and hold the college admission letters in your hands. Sit in a bus or a tractor and get to the city. After that it's you and your luck.'

The youth replied, 'Elders, it is our wish to do farming. Let the admission letter stay where it is. We will read all our books staying here. After a few days we will set up a computer learning centre. There are power cuts so often, so we will build our own generator. The terrain here is so hilly so we'll build check-dams. After the monsoon is over we will take a second crop, we will grow vegetables. We will educate our children ourselves by staying here in the village. The yield from the crops will increase. We can get back the jewellery mortgaged with the moneylender. During festivals we will sing and dance. The womenfolk know so many songs; we will listen to them. If outsiders come to impart wisdom to us then we will tell them, 'We are happy to listen to you. But you too must listen to what we have to say, Sir. We too have been thinking…'

Everyone was surprised. What was this! A fever never seen or heard of before had taken hold of their minds... All the youth replied in one voice 'This is the new outlook to development.'

VI

There was another village. This village used to get the benefit of each and every subsidy from the government. If the government floated some water-harvesting programmes, then immediately a hand pump would be made available in this village. Every year during the 'forest festival' new trees would be planted ritually by the Forest Department. Whenever the government officials planned a visit, they would make it a point to visit this village. Gradually it so happened that the farmers started to wait every year for the time when new plans and policies were announced. They knew that during a loan 'mela', eight or ten preferred persons from the village would surely get a loan. And there would be no consequences if they were unable to repay the loan. When the hand pump broke down there would be a fight between the persons whom the leaders favoured and those whom they did not favour. Gradually it so happened that the non-favoured persons didn't get anything while the favoured persons took away everything.

This continued for many years. But then the government itself had a shortage of funds. Then it was decided that every farmer had to pay for the electricity. It was also decided to end all subsides. There were no new benefit policies or plans and there was no path ahead.

The youth there said 'Now in this village the big question of earning daily bread has arisen. We should go to the city and find work there as labourers and earn a living for ourselves. It is better if the children and old people stay in the village itself.' These young men and women went off to the city. Even today we can see them toiling in every area of the city. But their children are still playing in the dirt and growing up without any hope of a better life.

VII

Development means thoughtfulness. Development means good sense. Without self-reliance, without standing on our own feet it is meaningless to even talk about development. The paucity of resources can always be reduced by thoughtfulness and good sense. Even if the land is rocky, it is possible to cultivate crops with the help of new agricultural techniques. Even if the rainfall is less or there is a shortage of water, it is possible to provide irrigation by hard work. Even when the subsidies coming from outside are cut down or stop completely, there can still be a sign of hope. If we are determined, it is possible to create a new life in one's own village itself. Everything is possible but one will have to work hard for it.

Nature is more important than humans. Society is more important than an individual. If an individual thinks first about the development of the society, then the individual's progress is also bound to happen at the same time. If we protect the environment, then we can solve human health problems. We have to think about all this. Development means to distinguish between good and bad.

To think or to share thoughts is not like daydreaming. Every village has different problems. For each one of these problems the solutions have to be found. If the problem is of debt then micro-finance schemes have to be created. Through these schemes one can surely become debt-free. If the problem is of water scarcity then we have to create a water harvesting cooperative. We have to build small dams. We will have to save every drop of rainwater. If the dowry amount is very high then all have to decide together to bring it down. If the red tape and bureaucracy in the government are affecting our plans we will have to work towards getting the wheels moving again. We must make the most of the government schemes that help us in making ourselves self-reliant. In every type of community work we must show honesty. We have to talk about every problem – with patience, courage and clarity.

Combining thoughtfulness and good sense means freeing ourselves from the addiction to bad habits. Bad habits are born from unreasonable thoughts. We should not be violent because the reason for violence is tangled thinking. We must reduce our wants in life because they increase the enmity and divisions between us. We must utilise time fruitfully because the time that passes never returns. We must treat every individual alike, as inequality between people is not conducive to development. Tribal villages must decide to abolish the caste system because injustice happens due to these differences.

How much will it cost to do all this? It will not cost a single rupee. By not doing all these things how much would we have to pay? As much as this so-called sophisticated world has paid, and a lot more.

VIII

I'll tell you a story.

There was a city. Dirty. Overflowing gutters. Illegal money existed in every home. The people there were very boastful and greedy. They were afraid of speaking the truth but could tell lies without hesitation. The city had big roads; and thousands of cars running on these roads contributed to the noise, pollution and dust.

Slowly the city started falling sick. The sickness would not let it sleep at night. The thought of the sins it had committed would startle it and wake it up at night. Because of that its hunger started increasing. No matter how much it ate; its hunger would not be satiated. Its favourite food was land. That is why the sick city started eating more and more land adjacent to it. The villages around it started falling sick.

Far away from this city, behind the mountains, there was an adivasi village. This was the same village whose youth had shared their vision with their elders. The village had now become self reliant. The city started calling out to the village, 'Why don't you join me? My hunger will not be assuaged until I consume you.'

Although the village was small it had a lot of self-confidence. So this village replied clearly, 'Brother, you are sick. Your sins have increased manifold. You won't be satisfied even after eating me. Listen to me. Learn something from me. I may be your younger sister, but I have earned the habit of hard work and my good sense through a lot of effort. I am willing to give them to you. With that your hunger and illness will both go away. From then on you will be freed from this sickness and insomnia.' The city felt that if by following the village, there was a possibility of getting well, then it should listen to what the village had to say.

So the city asked, 'My sister from the mountains, what are your new ideas?'

The adivasi village replied, 'The new idea is development'.

The city said, 'But that thing in plastic covers sent from America and England, isn't that development?'

The village replied, 'Big brother, what comes from outside, and is given as a loan, how can that be development? Development has to be initiated from within.

The city felt for the first time that perhaps there was a cure to its illness.

IX

Development means an increase in self-confidence, thoughts and ideas. We have to attain our goals all by ourselves. If we all become creative and start thinking for ourselves, then our villages too will be self-reliant and happy.

Everyone will have to start thinking of new methods for improving one's economy. We are either farmers, or if there is no farming then we are labourers. The question of irrigation for our crops will have to be solved without help from anyone. If four or five farmers get together, then even with their own labour, they will easily be able to dig a well. At the same time there are many experiments to try to collect rainwater and increase the level of water. It is important to get that information and to implement it. There is no cost to this; no one's permission is required. We can do it ourselves.

To keep our houses, our neighborhood and our villages clean is in our hands. To keep planting more and more trees, to water and nurture these plants is our duty. If all the men and women of a village get together and make this decision then in a span of two years the whole village will be lush green. There is no need for more water to do this. Using the drip system of irrigation, a few buckets of water per day is sufficient for every household to do all this. No one will come from outside to do this work. We will have to do it ourselves; we must do it ourselves.

It is very natural for conflicts to erupt within the village. But we will have to devise ways in which to resolve these conflicts so that we don't waste money on lawyers, courts and police. Besides whatever money we save from these legal pursuits can be used for the benefit of the village.

Every year we have to spend money to buy seeds, fertilisers and sprays. We can conveniently purchase these things wholesale if we get together. Everyone will also save a little money. Everyone should have the power to save, so that saving groups can extend loans in times of need. And slowly it will be possible to start small businesses and professions related to agriculture.

It is everyone's duty to ensure that each child in the village goes to school. If every child starts learning, then it will become a thoughtful individual, will be able to live and prosper in the contemporary world.

These are not small challenges. This is precisely what development is. No one's assistance is required to achieve this. Take this decision on your own. We will have to do this courageously. Only from seemingly minor achievements, will self-reliant homes, self-reliant villages, and a self-reliant country emerge.

Self-reliance is the only road to development. Once we make the decision to become self-reliant and try everything within our means to achieve it, it will not take long to achieve complete and holistic development. No political system in the world can stop us if we make this decision.

I suppose these thoughts from my adivasi friends will be beneficial to the larger world.

---

* *Vikas Vichar,* Translated from the Gujarati by Sarah Boltwalla and Kavita Patel

8
Reaching Out

In Pursuit of Success

Addiction is a psychological phenomenon and not a biological one. The origin of the addictive impulse is in the human brain. This is an accepted fact. Why is it then that other animals with relatively well-developed brains do not show a marked degree of the addictive impulse? The answer to that question lies, oddly enough, in the fact that the process of image-making is far more complex in the human brain than in that of other animals. Image-making and addiction are intimately related. It is the image-making ability of human beings that also makes possible in them the impulse to addiction. In order to understand this one needs to understand the processes of both image-making and addiction; and in order to understand addiction one must look not at the causes but the consequences of addiction.

The impact of any addictive material such as a drug or alcohol is hallucinatory. The degree of the illusion created may vary from substance to substance, but a temporary suspension of previously received imagery of the material world is a certainty. Under the spell of an addictive substance, a person experiences a significant rise in the dynamic quality of the natural and material phenomena. He/she feels excited, enthused, elated, empowered, starts seeing more colours and shapes, hears more sounds, tones and timbres. Probably, therefore, one may say that the psychological need to be under a spell arises out of the urge to experience a greater range of imagery than the human eye, memory and cognitive power can together offer to human intelligence.

Why is it that human intelligence alone, as far as we know, evinces the need to see this wide array of imagery? This is the same as asking why it is that the human animal alone craves to belong to a community stretching far beyond the immediate family? The answer to both these questions lies in a necessary stage in the process of the socialising of a human child described by psychologist Jacques Lacan as the 'mirror-stage'. During this stage the infant learns to perceive itself through the eyes of others, as if it looks at itself through the eyes of its own image in a mirror. This helps the infant to distinguish the subjective realm from the objective, to distinguish that which is 'itself' from all that is not 'itself'. The awareness of alterity and the emotions of shame, guilt, repentance — which are peculiarly human emotions — are rooted in this perception of the self as the other. The same perception paves a human infant's way to becoming a social animal. Similarly, the peculiarly human proclivity to addictive substance has its roots in this special human way of constructing the self-image.

What is known, as 'conscience' is in reality the ever-awake presence of the 'other world' looking at the inner, private emotional transactions of the self? When the conscience becomes too severe or restrictive, or when the self diverges too alarmingly from the expectations of the embedded 'other', it becomes necessary to violate the existing imagery— both of the self and of the external world. That is where hallucinatory experiences become inevitable. In most cases hallucinatory experiences are induced by chemicals generated within the human brain and the unconscious part of the psyche through the agency of dreams. But sleep and dreams may not suffice to protect the sensitivity of a person's self-image. The second degree of inducing hallucinatory imagery is achieved through a reconstruction of the imagery of the world through personalised and distorted verbal behaviour. This may result at the ordinary level in humour, hysteria or banter. At the higher level, it may result in a creative articulation such as acting, creation of fiction or poetry, or even yielding to silence and meditation. The third degree of image-making or reordering the placement of the self in relation to the non-self is achieved through aids that are external to the human physiology through drugs and addictive substances.

But there is another way of coming to terms with the pervasive pursuit of the self by the 'other' planted in the human consciousness during the mirror stage of maturation. And that way is reconstruction through appeasement. It is the method of telling a smart lie to oneself; in order to convince the self that the lie is indeed the truth, it needs to be told repeatedly. This amounts to saying that if one cannot change the world to suit one's own perception of it, it is better to mould one's self to suit the world's perception of oneself. The addiction to work and the pursuit of success are manifestations of this reverse psychic tendency.

There are two points of interest about this peculiarly human drive. The first is that though the successful in society (applying the commonly accepted yardstick of material achievement) are rarely in need of acquiring any further measure of such success for their biological preservation, in fact, they do not cease the quest to gain more and more. A rich man should feel less need to earn further. A powerful man should feel less fear of attack on his power by those who are not as powerful. But in reality we notice the converse happening. Riches only whet the appetite for more, and power breeds the fear of loss of that power. The second point is that all those who are considered successful tend to become increasingly orthodox in that they start opposing any ideas of change.

These two tags, permanently attached to material success, are the inevitable machinery of the smart lie that the self tells the perpetually alert 'other'. To speak metaphorically, these persons start sleeping with their boots on. Actually, they do not sleep at all even when their bodies go through the motions of physical sleep. Materially successful individuals are in the act of eternally escaping from their selves. They can never really rest. Therefore, they must chase further success, even after becoming successful. This is how workaholics are made. Workaholics are like tigers that have tasted human blood; having tasted it they can never go back to their natural diet. In all likelihood, the maneater is not an exemplar in the community of tigers. However, in human society, the successful workaholic is not only valued but even overvalued and the parameters for assessing success are restricted to the material ones.

Labour has come to be stratified in terms of the non-productive and the productive, as well as that which is convertible to capital. Those who manage this completely unnatural conversion, those who succeed in building up capital are seen as successful. Those who are the real achievers, not just for themselves but also for the human race, are normally those who are far from successful in this limited sense. The thinkers, the revolutionaries, the prophets, the inventors have, more often than not, been those who have tasted and lived not with success, but with failure. It is said of Shakespeare that his greatness lay in the fact that he never exploited his own success. Someone of the calibre of James Joyce is seen as the writer's writer precisely because he knew how to explore the farthest verge of the failure of language. And neither Jesus Christ nor Mahatma Gandhi can be put down in the category of successful persons. They were great mainly because they were aware of their own vulnerability and weakness and were willing to fail.

The addicts who seek solace in drug- induced hallucinatory imagery are psychologically weak. But those who pursue the path of material success even when such achievement is not necessary for meeting their biological needs, are weaker still. The *Bhagwad Gita* understood how ephemeral and how non-creative is their drive to realise the self. Therefore, the two most persuasive injunctions the *Gita* offers are, one, detaching action from its acquisitional impulse, and two, unveiling the self so as to disengage it from the tyranny of definition by others. In the ultimate analysis it is only apparently an irony that those whom the world considers successful are the failed ones, and those who are prepared to face failure are the true creators. However, the fear of unleashing the world— the other— on the self is so threatening that most of us either turn to drugs or try to chase success. And because such a large number of human animals are engaged in that pursuit, rarely do we muster up the courage and honesty to call society's bluff, leaving that burden to the seers and the prophets.

Yet there is another kind of success, another kind of pursuit.

The human brain, both as a collective property of the human species as well as the neurological aggregate of an individual, is an ever-developing entity. A community uses it to enter into a more complete negotiation with natural phenomena; an individual uses it to sharpen physical skills. This process of excelling oneself, a process which may have nothing to do with the acquisitive drive, satisfies one's pride in being oneself. Many of those who are addicted to success are driven by the desire to excel in their own field of activity or skill. Therefore those who are truly successful are never content with their past accomplishments. There is only one direction to which their faces are permanently turned, and that is the future. No writer ever thinks that he has already written his best work; no sportsman ever thinks that he has already played his best game. In such cases the intellect and the body are driving each other to the extreme verge of possibility. One may therefore say that the addiction to success, when it is not born out of the desire to escape censure, is caused by the irresistible inquisitiveness for exploring the abyss of failure.

A Thought For The Dispossessed

In the village school that I attended, one of the teachers had inscribed in matchless calligraphy, 'Early to bed, early to rise/Makes man healthy, wealthy and wise'. I grew up reading this sentence every day. It took me several decades to realise that apart from its bad grammar, the sentence was quite untruthful. Indeed health, wealth and wisdom have no logical interconnections, and one who has attained wisdom will hardly care for health and much less for wealth. However, the realisation did not come from my layman's knowledge of the lives of saints and prophets. It dawned slowly and imperceptibly; but a sudden light was shed while I was reading John Ruskin's classic *Unto This Last.*

This great book, which influenced Mahatma Gandhi's thought so profoundly, contains a little story. A certain merchant had amassed gold. The ship started sinking while he was sailing to another country. He had therefore to dive into the sea with all his gold. But the burden of gold took him straight to the bottom of the sea. Ruskin asks, at this point, a self-answering question: 'Did the man get the gold, or the gold get the man?'

Ruskin's story is of course told in the historical context of the notorious gold rush in the American continent causing in its wake the rise of a trigger-happy generation of picaros. In that world the avarice for gold made human life an insignificant token. Saints and sinners are pretty certain in their attitudes to wealth. But wealth has been a major dilemma for everyone else.

First and foremost, if health and even wisdom are universally desired attributes of the animate world, wealth seems to have been the desire only of humankind. It is impossible to say as to when and how this desire entered the ecology of human emotions. The instinct to gather may have been inherited by homo sapiens from bees and ants that gather honey and food. But the stage beyond hunting and gathering, in which the ideas of property and possession become important, belongs peculiarly to human history.

In the early stages of the prehistory of the human race, one important invention was the use of pointed weapons and instruments made out of rock splinters. These created the possibility of using violence imaginatively, and beyond the minimum need for hunting and self-defence. Probably, the earliest form of such use of violence —not directed to other animals but directed to other homo sapiens —was used for minimising labour. Those who could display and use violence and build up a stock of weapons could live without having to labour at hunting, gathering, or producing. They could accumulate wealth without having to do a corresponding amount of physical work. Thus the earliest forms of wealth made a delinking of labour and possession an implicit requirement. It also made the use of violence, in whatever form, an attendant prerequisite for any accumulation of wealth. For a long time wealth and its actual material representations, such as food, cattle, silver and gold, were used for the purpose of exchange between labour and violence, by the dispossessed and the one in possession. But this direct and equal exchange was replaced by the exchange of a mere imagery of wealth when collective human labour had extracted a lot more from nature than its collective needs. Thus glass beads, bits of leather, wooden or metal seals, colourful objects and finally printed paper came to represent wealth. As social relationships grew complex and economic relations became essentially alienated from emotional relationships, the standardisation of the imagery of wealth became inevitable. And of course the state, as the most violent of legal entities in a given society, took over this function. Since then, though individuals and the society as a whole produce wealth and consume it, the regulation of wealth, its circulation and exchange came to be the sole prerogative of the state. And in exchange for exercising this privilege, the state also acquired the authority and power to collect a part of wealth that individuals (or the society as a whole) generated.

Given that violence, authority and power lie at the root of the generation of excess wealth and its regulation within a social framework, two kinds of profound inequalities seem to have emerged in human history. The first is the unequal power relation between the state and any single member citizen. The second is the inequality between those who inherit and control wealth and those who may generate it but do not control it.

The classical debates on the concept of wealth—both national and individual, at the beginning of the industrial revolution tried to focus on the nature of the inequality between the individual and the state. The Marxist interpretation of wealth focussed on both the inequalities. The more idealistic versions pointed to the spiritual content of the human person and imagined that a trusteeship attitude of active non-attachment may be a possibility. It is indeed possible to defend all three positions on the basis of actual behaviour of human beings; and therefore, it is impossible to accept any of the three as exclusively defensible. What may probably be pointed out is that the states that succeed in regulating wealth effectively also tend to acquire a greater ability to be violent. Not surprisingly, in the contemporary world the wealthy are not known by their display of wealth but by the cordon of armed security that seal them off from the rest of the world.

Thus at the end of a long history of evolution, the imagery of wealth has returned to where it all began. No longer do the glass-bead, silver bit, gold coin, silk and saffron, cattle and horses, cars and penthouses announce to the world the fact of being wealthy. In order to be known as really, really wealthy one must be surrounded by the ultramodern versions of the primitive rock flints. And even while we are all made to believe that the market is taking over the state, the exchange of wealth must be carried out in the secrecy and the anonymity of cyberspace. Now begins the second age of the history of wealth, which threatens to leave out the real markets of real things for the dispossessed as once long ago, it eliminated real labour for the rich. That thought is cold compensation for the dispossessed.

Transition Forever

That change is the only permanent truth of life seems to have been the ultimate conclusion of all human experience. Nature changes, from season to season as well as from place to place. The body changes from moment to moment. Human society changes from one historical epoch to another epoch. Ibsen believed that even Truth changes every eight or ten years. It is an old philosophical question as to whether one can stand in the same river twice, because even though the stream may seem to be the same, the water in it is not the same. Transition, therefore, is recognised as the ultimate and absolute condition of existence.

Yet the human mind seems to agitate against change in every possible manner. An enormous amount of our psychic energy has been expended in every age and every clime in conceptualising a gigantic machinery of the absolute and the imperishable. If sensory experience tells reason that change is the essence of existence, the imagination keeps creating various notions of the changeless. This dialogue between the *kshara* and the *akshara* pervades all areas of human activity, sacred and secular, private and social, natural and cultural.

One does not know when or why man posited the notion of

god. However, in whatever form this notion is manifest— personified, impersonal, totemic or as energy, etc— the divine is universally recognised as free from the natural laws of transition. In fact, to find an escape from the condition of perpetual transition seems to have been the ideal set before human beings by various religions. This ideal, which every human being knows is never attainable, seems to fulfil the profound craving to bring the natural process of change to an irrevocable halt.

At the back of the sensory perception of transition is the philosophical notion of time. Had man not created and acknowledged time, there was no possibility of perceiving transition of any kind at all. Philosophers have debated from very ancient times whether time is created by human cognition or it exists independent of human cognition as an autonomous phenomenon, whether it is absolute in essence or merely relative. However, these are, without exception, only philosophical positions with axiomatic value. They can be debated upon but cannot be proved as scientific truth or dismissed as errors in thought. The truth of the matter is that the body, and therefore human consciousness, is trapped within so much that is 'the other', including the phenomenal world, that the human mind has to conceptualise reference points that are at least notionally permanent, to map out the field of consciousness. Time and space are the two universally employed reference points. Once time is conceptualised, the perception of transition becomes an inevitable corollary.

Yet, the concept of time by itself cannot account for the perception of transition. Whether a notion of time existed or not, the body is bound to grow old in its progression from birth to death. Similarly, matter and all material objects, go through a cycle of manifestation and dissolution. Cosmic and celestial phenomena too clearly show histories of creation and decline. And finally, communities and larger social groups change over time.

One likes to believe that it was as an escape from the fear of dissolution, death and the inexorable flux that the ancient Greek philosophers conceptualised the ideal world. In the ideal world of Plato and Aristotle, all worldly objects had a model, the original single idea of which the worldly objects are perishable and inadequate copies. This duality between the Ideal and the Actual provided the context for Aristotle's theory of mimesis, a theory of transition that can derive its sanctity only from the intransient.

In Indian philosophy too, the concepts of stillness and poise are given the most central place. The highest knowledge is where all cognition dissolves into *shanti*, the peace that passes all understanding. It is the condition where the mental apparatus of perceiving change transmutes and submits itself to a detachment par excellence, which will then relegate the transient into the realm of the non-real. Indian philosophy, even of the atheistic school, expected the highest sensory enjoyment, the aesthetic, to culminate in the *shanta rasa*. Critics like Abhinavagupta tell us that after all the turmoil of the epoch-making war in the *Mahabharata*, the epic really derives its greatness from its capacity to evoke the *shanta rasa*. The Upanishads and the *Gita* spend a considerable amount of philosophical thought describing the *akshara*, the imperishable principle completely unaffected by transition. Thus, from very ancient times the dichotomy between the knowledge of transition collected by the senses and the desire to free the mind from fragmented existence have occupied the central place in man's encounter with existence.

The prerogative to conceptualise eternal Time is not the philosopher's alone. Ordinary people, throughout human history, have agitated against the transience of the body and matter by actively generating folklore related to immortality and eternity. In this universal space of folklore reside all our ghosts, genii, snakes that live for centuries, nymphs, gnomes, *rakshasas*, *gandharvas*, and all para-psychic beings that defy the laws of death. In fact, the unconscious is at once gripped by the fear of death, even the mysterious wish for death, as well as being gifted with the ability to churn out dreams of immortality. Among lesser mortals such dreams are sustained through a process of subscribing to the collective fund of myths, legends and folklore about immortality. For those who are seen as strong persons, they are internalised so that these persons strive to attain immortality through their actions. The most serious challenge to this wish-fulfilment comes, however, not from the intellect that knows its impossibility but from the nature of social organisation.

The needs of the body such as hunger, sleep and sexual desire create man's dependence on other human beings. The ability to use language, and the unique shape and functioning of the human brain create the possibility of the articulation and formalising of human interdependence. Family, clan, community, society are the progressive stages of this articulation and formalisation. These social structures inevitably give rise to structures of authority and power. In their turn, such structures of authority tend to result in the distribution of patterns of labour necessary for survival and defence. And finally, that distribution generates within the human mind the desire to change the established hierarchies of power. Each step is logically connected with the other. The total result is that, unlike other animal species, the human species shows a marked craving for social mobility. Revolutions are brought about, wars are fought, history is made and also continuously unmade, and technologies are developed — all out of this very basic craving for effecting social mobility. In fact, progress and change are seen as positive social values by all human societies.

Thus, if the religious and philosophical ideals for man postulate the intransient and the immortal as the highest order of being, the political and social ideals for man sing the glories of change and dynamism. Human life is caught between these two, between the knowledge accumulated by the senses and that imbued from intuition, between the political and the religious. Nowhere else does this conflict come through as dramatically as in John Milton's epic *Paradise Lost*. In it, Christ is the poetic figure for the intransient, the immortal and the eternal. As against this, Satan is the prophet of political change and historical dynamism. Satan causes the beginning of human history, saddled with unconscious desires and sensory experience. Christ redeems man from it, making him free from the terror of transience. Milton found both these figures heroic. To choose between politics and religion was as difficult in his times as it is in ours.

This impossible choice is the very condition of the human

existence. It may be possible for a Savitri to bring a Satyavan back from the arms of death, or an Orpheus to lure a Euridice away from it. It may be possible for an artist to think of a phoenix that will defy the laws of nature altogether. However, the logic of the human body, the history of its genes, and the time-space bind within which it lives, make transition an inescapable reality. The nature of the social organisation and its innate political wisdom make transition not only inevitable but also even desirable. The fear of death, and the body's attachment to itself and to the material world, makes transition a feared and oppressive thought. The clash between these various pulls on man's senses and mind make human existence what it is. We need them all: the longing for transition, the desire to re-order the manifest world, the intuition of the permanent and the yearning to possess the entirety of experience by more than mere senses.

The Moving Spirit

The dichotomy between the human body, made of perishable material, and human consciousness, which is apparently free to transcend the limits of space and time, has been one of the central forces that create cultural dynamics. All art and creativity spring from the conflict between the two, all spirituality wells up from that source. The search for that which transcends the material world then takes on a variety of forms. Sometimes it turns to the symbols of worship, at other times to devotion to human messengers of the eternal. But while symbols of eternity, human or otherwise, become the medium for spiritual yearning, the yearning itself is firmly located in the human body. Therefore, a certain degree of control over the body, putting it through some tradition-bound regime of spiritual exercise, becomes an essential part of the realisation of that longing. That in essence is the motivation for the age-old custom of pilgrimage.

It is just not possible to determine how old this tradition is. But we notice that pilgrimages are recorded in the ancient literature and scriptures of all cultures. In our tradition, we find elaborate descriptions of pilgrimages not only in the epics but also as an inevitable beginning of every prose narrative, whether the Jatakas, the *Kathasaritasagar* or the Puranas. The destinations may vary from the Himalayas, various hermitages, holy cities, shrines, natural mysteries and scenic spots. But the motif remains the most archetypal component of the growth and transaction of the human mind. In European literature too are found many references to pilgrimages, whether in Homer, Dante or Chaucer. And the most fascinating pilgrim stories of the world come from the Islamic world, from Arabic and Persian literature. In the Judeo-Christian tradition, Dante's *Divine Comedy* and Bunyan's *Pilgrim's Progress* are probably the ultimate literary expressions (in poetry and prose respectively) of the pervasive and profound desire for spirituality.

However, it is the picaresque mode of writing that grapples with the driving force behind the hunger for a spiritual quest. This mode of writing, which first developed in Spain and France, shows a fascinating interest in the moral aspects of spiritual journeys. The hero, known as a picaro, a vagabond, free of moral scruples, learns the value of love as a Christian value through his encounters with the world of crime and deceit. Thus, picaresque fiction takes into account the material side of the dichotomy between the body and the mind that spurs the urge for pilgrimage.

Yet, it will be far from correct to say that the purpose of pilgrimages is only spiritual. The history of pilgrimage shows that, probably, the purpose is aesthetic as well as ethical and spiritual. The long walks and the lonely halts were probably intended to provide opportunities to release the fatigue caused by the familiar. Staying with strangers and sharing food and rituals with them were perhaps aimed at relieving the ego of the excesses of self-consciousness. Through these release mechanisms, the sensory perceptions were given a chance to regain their sharpness so that the world experienced by them becomes enjoyable once again. Hence, it is the ritual value of pilgrimages that has a greater significance. Through these rituals is enhanced the collective well-being of communities.

One such ritual pilgrimage is the *vari* in Maharashtra. The destination of the pilgrims is the ancient temple town of Pandharpur. The deity there is Vithoba, variant of Vishnu, but the entire pilgrimage is woven around the saint tradition of Maharashtra. The Pandharpur *vari* is clearly a folk ritual. It accommodates persons from all castes, classes, age groups and professions. Even non-Hindu tribals and Muslims take part in it. It takes place in the months of Ashadh and Kartik. The route of the pilgrimage starts at Alandi, the place associated with the thirteenth century poet-saint Jnaneshwar. It passes through Jejuri, which is the temple town most sacred for Dhangars, a nomadic tribal community. The conclusion of the pilgrimage is marked by a ritual dip in the river Chandrabhaga, called so because of its crescent bed in Pandharpur. All along the route, villagers welcome the pilgrims and serve them food. The pilgrims themselves organise small *bhajan* groups and sing and dance to the tune of those songs. All songs are recalled and recited from the writings of the saints like Namdev, Tukaram, Chokhamela and Janabai. Invariably, the pilgrims are clad in spotless white. The number swells as they approach Pandharpur at the end of the fifteen-day march, often crossing the mark of half a million. The sight of such a mass of humanity, neatly distributed in *bhajan* groups, tuned to the eternity of the great literary works in Marathi, Hindi and Kannada, is so hypnotising that no *varkari* ever returns home without shedding his or her anxieties and stress. Thus a kind of therapeutic hypnotism is effected by pilgrimages bringing in a sense of well being for the peasant and artisan communities of Maharashtra.

But for those who take up pilgrimages, there may be an entirely personal reason such as a vow made or a desire to seek blessings, or even to achieve a sense of equanimity by bowing to a symbolic manifestation of the divine. The *yatras* to the *maths* and *lingas* in the Himalayas, the Hajj to Mecca and Medina, the retreats sought in monasteries by Christian and Buddhist monks have such motivations. There is always the need for every person to submit to a force, which is larger than the self and cosmic in significance. Pilgrimages help fulfil that desire. One may say that the feminine in the psyche is at the root of the desire for a spiritual journey. Pilgrimages become increasingly necessary in closely organised societies faced by the prospect of the increasing severity of the state machinery. The modern State, with its army, its legal system based on reason, the parliament regulated by the strength of political parties promotes the masculine side of the psyche and creates the wherewithal for its full gratification, almost in excess of its own desire. And so, the feminine aspects too must find a release and articulation through rituals, hypnosis, frenzied dance and songs, self-denial of an ascetic type and a certain masochism. Pilgrimages provide an opportunity for all these. In a way, modern-day 'tourism' and the strong and even 'self-destructive' longing for holidays are but a secular version of the older forms of pilgrimage. In this version sea-beaches and pubs, theatre and poolrooms replace shrines and rivers, sacred groves and the icons of the earlier times. Yet, it cannot be denied that the cultural practice of pilgrimage is closely linked with the sense of the well being of a community. It offers the pilgrim a certain opportunity of entering into a new subjectivity, giving the human consciousness, once again, the ability to enter into a new relationship with the body as well as the world surrounding it. It is, in the ultimate analysis, the most public and the most articulate expression of returning to the mother's womb, a primeval search for innocence. Pilgrimage therefore is the journey, to use William Blake's expression, from the darkness of experience to the song of innocence.

Rivers Forever

When you stand in a river for the second time, is it the same river in which you stood earlier? This is an old philosophical question, which has no explanation that is logical as well as convincing. Philosophers formulate the question in order to bring out the ceaseless dynamism of natural phenomena. But it is also posed to state through a metaphor the paradoxical relationship between eternity and change. No metaphor other than that of a river could have served this purpose as effectively, for it epitomises at once, all that is timeless and all that is ephemeral in human existence.

It is a river alone that allows the human mind to grasp eternity through a direct and intimate physical experience. The celestial bodies are eternal; yet we can but see them without ever being able to touch them. It took man several thousand years of efforts to determine the exact physical locations of the planetary system. The moon came within our physical grasp only about a few decades ago; and the sun will remain outside it for all human time to come. But the rivers have been with us from the beginning of human memory. The music of their flowing has sung the cradle-songs of human civilisation on every continent. And rivers have been for man a perennial symbol of the timeless.

Another reason for the importance of rivers in man's spiritual perception of the world is that they make no demand on human labour. Food and water are necessary for the survival of the species. But, in order to get food, animals have to be hunted, land has to be cultivated, the hunted and the gathered have to be roasted or boiled. As against this, rivers need neither be chased, nor cultivated. They offer water ready to drink round the year. Naturally, therefore, human beings have always thought of them in terms of kindness incarnate. And since rivers demand no labour from us in exchange for what they give us, they — together with air— remained for a considerably long period in the making of human civilisation, outside the network of economic exchange. The turning point came when, with the rise of nationalism, rivers, together with land, started being perceived as national property and therefore, exchangeable economic entities.

Considering the material importance of rivers in human existence and their total independence from human labour, it is not surprising that they are vested with an enormous spiritual significance. Temples are built on their banks. Cities that have grown up along the banks are considered holy cities; pilgrimages are made to such temples and cities, and river festivals are celebrated in different seasons. However, the spiritual significance of rivers is restricted to the purificatory and does not extend to the creational. It is interesting to note that no river is given the credit for creating the universe. That credit is reserved for the unseen or the abstract, either godhead or an energy, which is not materially manifest, such as sound. Rivers have to be content with washing the sins of human beings, allowing gods to bathe, or hosting abandoned children who will grow up to become great heroes. At best, rivers can be populated with the creatures of our fantasy world such as fairies and snake-gods. One can say that in the kingdom of myth, if the skies are vested with the glory of the grand narrative of the creation and destruction of the universe, rivers are painted with the colours of folklore. This is so mainly because of the material intimacy of rivers with human life. We drink river water, draw it for irrigation, have a ritual dip in it, or swim across it to the other bank. Rivers are never invisible, never non-negotiable. They are present before us all the time; and their presence is even more substantial than that of mountains or land because of the fluid and dynamic material texture of their being.

The spiritual qualities associated with rivers are those of the mother, not of the father; they are feminine more than masculine. The rivers therefore form the soft lap and not the tough sinews of the body of myths constructed by the human imagination. Accordingly, our relation with rivers is intensely emotional. Songs of haunting beauty and tales of mystery, involvement and separation articulate this relationship.

One may say that just as a part of man's spiritual being is shaped by looking up to the temple-towers, mountain-peaks and the skies, another part of that being is shaped by looking at the flowing rivers, that alternate between monsoon fury and the summer calm. It is more of the narcissistic part of the personality that the river-element controls, the altruistic being guided by the skies. It is not surprising therefore, that in the story of Narcissus and Echo, the mythological hero is believed to have learnt how handsome he was by looking at his reflection in the clear waters of a river.

Probably the river that showed Narcissus his reflection has much to regret now. At the beginning of the nineteenth century Wordsworth could enjoy the calm serenity of the Thames welcoming the dawn. But a century later T.S. Eliot found that the Thames was probably weeping to see the desolation surrounding it. The narcissistic tendency of the human race, which initially triggered off the acquisitive urge, has now come to entrap us from all sides in the form of a mindless devastation of nature. Rivers, even the mightiest among them such as the Nile, the Amazon and the Ganga, have been reduced to sewage dumps and are rapidly becoming culturally inert bodies. The stench that rises from their befouled bodies is so terrible that the delicate poetry and folklore associated with them are hardly meaningful to us.

In the *Mahabharata*, the Ganga has been the most fertile and benevolent mother, almost the breast giver to the human race. Today, we have turned it to a condition which reminds us of the story 'Breast-Giver' by the Bangla writer Mahasweta Devi, which is about a much-pimped, much-tormented tribal woman. The plight of the smaller rivers is even worse. Most of them have come to be only seasonal rivers. Their job seems to be to drain the monsoon water and to remain parched during the rest of the year.

One had not heard of river-water disputes till about the middle of the twentieth century. There had been wars for control over rivers as navigational routes in the countries that are land-locked on all sides. But the commodification of river water is a recent phenomenon; and this phenomenon is irreversible. Similarly, there used to be food-riots in the past; but riots for river water are of recent origin. And possibly, rivers and the distribution of their waters will become one of the most politicised of ecological issues. In the process, what traditionally belonged to the sphere of the Divine will be taken over by the sphere of the State. There is, of course, no going back into history and myth. But, at least keeping the rivers alive and clean is the minimum that we must do to pay back our historical debts to the rivers that have given us, over the millennia, the love that mothers, and the life that goddesses alone can give.

Reaching Out

Why a person gives up the comforts of a normal life and starts working for the betterment of the community is quite a mystery. Legends may ascribe this mysterious desire to certain dramatic moments of realisation; but to believe that a Mahatma is motivated to dedicate himself to the cause of freedom merely because he is thrown out of a South African train is to give too much credit to mere outer circumstances. We know that there are innumerable persons who are subjected to injustice everywhere and every day. But only rarely does one of them give up his self-centered existence and take to an altruistic mode of life. Besides, not everyone who does so has had to face a mind-shattering, agonising experience. There are some theories of the link between goodness and divine inspiration. It is believed that a special touch of divine inspiration turns human beings into saints. This belief is strengthened because often, though not invariably, we see god-men doing work that shows the quality of goodness. But it would be worth considering if this theory is tenable beyond the realm of faith. In fact, one may notice on a closer scrutiny that it is their goodness that bestows sainthood on the saints and allows us to conceptualise the divine. What appears as the consequence, therefore, is really the cause of what appears as the cause. It is of course true that those who possess goodness disown it by ascribing its origin to their faith in a power, which is superior to the human mind. But that should be taken as a measure of their moral commitment to altruism as a way of life.

Religious philosophies have another way of explaining goodness, particularly those philosophies which privilege a single prophet as the representative of god. In their account, goodness is a pre-human and perennial force eternally poised against an opposite force such as evil, and human existence and history are the predestined battleground for the two to prove their might. Such philosophies imply that the freedom that the human mind has to create its own forces is limited to making choices alone, whether metaphysical or existential.

If we were to think of the human mind differently, as Sigmund Freud did, we would have to think of goodness as a twin not of evil but of self-centredness. Modern psychology is inclined to interpret a person's desire to do something beyond the call of the person's self-perseverance as a result of the individual's self-perception. This amounts to saying that one engages in acts of goodness in order to protect one's own image as a goodness agent. It is pointless to argue that whereas psychology offers us excellent insights into the essential nature of violence, greed, guilt, erotic desires, jealousy and possessiveness, it does not prove of much help in understanding compassion, helpfulness, nobility of thought and other 'good' emotions. This discipline developed out of the need to treat mentally 'irregular' persons and therefore it has spent most of its energies analysing socially dangerous and physically undesirable drives. Therefore 'goodness' is not something that modern psychology can explain satisfactorily.

Such being the present condition of our knowledge about altruism, we have to rest content merely with describing it in a subjective and tentative way. As such it may help to look at some examples.

When there is a national calamity such as a war, everybody is prepared to make sacrifices. If the calamity is caused by the fury of nature, such as an earthquake, cyclone, floods or volcanic outbursts, we notice that even those outside the national boundaries are prepared to make sacrifices and help the victims of such calamities. These are special moments when communities rediscover their benumbed sensitivity. Nature's fury sends us a reminder of how fragile and easily perishable human civilisation is; and we instinctively participate in restoring our claim to a continued existence by helping those in distress. Such goodness is born partly out of fear and partly out of pity and is almost like the experience of Tragedy described by Aristotle. It quickens our sensitivity momentarily but is not long lasting.

There is another manifestation of 'goodness' that we notice among individuals working in the social sphere. In this manifestation the goodness drive is sustained over a long period. It does not remain merely as emotional energy but also acquires the form of rational constructs. Such individuals, and the groups they form, start explaining the need for doing good deeds in terms of objectives that will lead to a better human habitation. Hence we have individuals or groups fighting for social justice and helping the oppressed and the destitute. There is, often, in such work an element of acquisition of moral authority if not social prestige. The moral authority that individuals gain out of the community work they do possesses a certain degree of permanence. Unlike political authority it does not depend on any social mandate, and unlike money power it cannot be wrested away through competition. Therefore, it allows the individual an immense freedom for creative self-expression. However, this freedom can be understood only through a direct personal experience. It cannot be described, expect in terms of metaphor. The English Romantic poet Shelley wrote:

> I can give not what men call love
> But wilt thou accept not what the heart lifts above and the heavens reject not
> The desire of the moth for the star, of the night for the morrow
> A longing for something afar from the sphere of our sorrow

This desire to belong to a dream realm far from the sphere of our animal world is the source of goodness that individuals display in every society and age. The creative freedom that their sacrifice and dedication brings in return is the intoxicating energy that fuels their resolve to change human existence. At the heart of goodness is the limitless freedom, which allows the human to be divine.

9

The Song of Orpheus

I

Long ago, not in historical ages but in mythical aeons, Orpheus waged a struggle to bring his beloved Eurydice back from the kingdom of Death. Death promised to return Eurydice to Orpheus, on condition that as she followed his footsteps, he would not turn his head back to see if she was really following him. As Orpheus emerged out of the world of darkness, on the sheer strength of his faith that Eurydice was indeed following him, he kept composing poems that he sang aloud. The music was meant for communicating with Eurydice the great turmoil and passion in his heart; it was meant to express the joy of having brought his beloved back to life; it was also meant to overcome the anxiety in Orpheus's mind that after all Eurydice may not be following him at all. It is said that a million birds followed Eurydice entrapped by his divine music. It was music to their ears; but for Orpheus, his song was at once a cry of agony and a proclamation of faith! That song of Orpheus is heard echoed in every single act of every pioneer.

II

Human imagination has felt perennially fascinated by the natural processes of creation, preservation and destruction. From ancient times, there have been mythological, literary and iconographic representations of man's engagement with these processes. In Indian iconographic tradition, the spirit of sustenance is represented by the figure of Vishnu reclining on the coils of an aquatic-serpentine Ananta or Shesha. Vishnu is considered the supporter of Space, Shesha, the supporter of Time, and in their togetherness is the interlocking of Space and Time. Heinrich Zimmer's comment (in his book *Myths and Symbols in Indian Art and Culture*) on this representation is:

> Vishnu sleeps like a spider that has climbed up the thread that once issued from its own organism, drawing it back into itself, the god has consumed again the web of the universe. Alone upon the immortal substance of the ocean, a giant figure, submerged partly, partly afloat, he takes delight in slumber. There is no one to behold him, no one to comprehend him; there is no knowledge of him, except within himself.

But, if there are archetypes of creation and sustenance in all civilisations, there are also the myths and archetypes of change and destruction. If in one story it is the post-lapserian Eve and Adam who must toil and hurt Mother Earth to eke out a living, in another it is the great warrior Karna, the master of superb weapons, whose chariot gets stuck in the middle of the battle-field immobilising him. Such myths indicate that to be human is to struggle, to strive for what is unattainable, with the knowledge that the unceasing human endeavour often produces a condition of life that is even more dehumanising than before. The desire for changing our collective destinies too has been a perennial feature of the human psyche. The dialectics between continuity and change, disillusionment and optimism, and conservation and innovation too is a permanent feature of human thought. Those who want to change the world, to innovate it, to re-invent it, say, 'but why not?' Those who feel disillusioned and wish to cling to the deadwood say, 'Why at all?' True sustenance and a genuine conservation, therefore, must be distinguished from cynicism and apathy.

The great compassion of the prophet of Galilee results in the hammering of nails on the cross; Rome's majesty and grandeur ends up in a masquerade of barbarians; all the holy Crusades spawn marauding mercenaries; the lofty ideals of a French Revolution deliver nothing but the tyranny of a Napoleon; the might of the industrial revolution is usurped by a dehumanising colonialism; and the high songs of the workers' equality and freedom freeze into a Kremlin bureaucracy: the cynic, therefore, may say, 'Why go through it all? Why crave for change when history shows again and again that every change will carry within it the seeds of an unprecedented man-made disaster? Why strive for it if at the end one is forced to say with the Irish poet William Butler Yeats, "Everything changed, changed utterly, a terrible beauty is born." '

The myth that encapsulates the futility of change, progress and development is the myth of Sisyphus. His hands are tied in chains, and yet he must continue to serve his perennial sentence of pushing a huge boulder from the bottom to the top of a mountain. He does so, putting in heroic toil; but every time the boulder gets close to the mountain top, it comes tumbling down. Sisyphus must start all over again, yet another chapter in his endless sentence.

The modern French thinker Albert Camus was fascinated by this myth which traditionally signified the absurdity of human will and which he presented in his book. *The Myth of Sisyphus.* Camus, however, had another view about human will. In a novel called *The Plague*, Camus presents a fictional structure to his philosophy of action. In the novel, Dr Reaux finds himself entrapped in a city struck by an epidemic. No one knows the why and the wherefore of the plague that has hit the city of Oran. Everybody panics and tries to find an escape route. The citizens queue up for visas, and, when the city is cordoned off, they are prepared to pay bribes for an exit. The priest pontificates claiming that God's wrath had been visited upon His erring children and so they must now reaffirm their affiliation to the church. Dr Rieux however, neither escapes the physical space of Oran nor the moral responsibility of the here and now. He keeps working for the dying patients and merely states, 'I will do as much as I can'. The epidemic subsides as mysteriously as it had erupted. Doctor Rieux, however, has the moral satisfaction that he has not fled Oran in the face of the absurd.

Whether or not the world changes because of an individual's efforts, whether or not the phenomenal cosmic reality surrounding us responds to our desires and aspirations, one must work to change the world and make it more humane, more compassionate, more beautiful. There is no point in throwing up one's hands in doubt as the young prince Hamlet did when he cried out, 'The time is out of joint, oh cursed spite, that I was ever born to set it right.' Perhaps, every generation in every age must say with the poet Shelley, 'Hope, till Hope creates the thing it contemplates!' And, even if, we must carry on our backs the curse given to Orpheus, Sisyphus, Karna and Adam that repeatedly shatters our dreams, we should have the resilience to proclaim, 'Like a child from the womb, like a ghost from the tomb, I will rise and build them again.' The challenge of being human is the challenge of sustaining our hope that someday this world will have universal freedom, universal equality and global peace.

II

If freedom, equality and peace have as yet remained unfulfilled ideals in a genuinely universal sense, it is not because the very nature of these notions is perpetually progressive, or because attempts have not been made in this direction. Human history is full of instances of such attempts from the hoary philosophers of the Upanishads to Mahatma Gandhi in the east and from Socrates to Martin Luther King in the west. One feels that if the world were to follow the ideals of even one thinker or activist belonging to the order of Gautam Buddha, Karl Marx, Nelson Mandela, all would be achieved. The problem is not that we are short of ideas, ideals and idealism, it is rather that of the immense complexities in the transactions of daily life, the burden of fractured and charred historical memories, the intricacies of the desires of greed, hatred and destruction and the obsessive human engagement in the self. The family, the ethnic identity, blind us to the great insights offered by the visionaries. Their insights and our blindness have continued to conflict. Their sacrifice and our greed have continued to quarrel.

Arthur Koestler, one of the most remarkable historians of ideas, devoted considerable attention to the question of civilisation shifts. In his memorable book *The Yogi and the Commissar* he observed that societies do not respond either to the spiritual allurement of a saint or to the political bulldozing of a Tsar. On the colour spectrum of the human emotions and aspirations, Koestler put the Tsar at the infra-red extreme and the saint at the ultra-violet extreme. He maintained that a civilisational change, in order to be lasting, must come from the grey areas in between the two extremes. In other words, values like freedom, equality and peace will be universally stabilised in human affairs not because they are offered to us by great philosophers, saints, revolutionaries, or popes, or governments and institutions. They will be stabilised only if they take root in the consciousness of the ordinary, the faceless and the nameless, and find hospitable shelter in the hearts of each one of us. Let me hasten to add that considering the long history of human beings from their original animal status to a condition of being truly civilised this change is bound to occur very slowly, almost imperceptibly and in miniscule steps. But it is these small, imperceptible steps that matter. Mahatma Gandhi believed that his little spinning wheel was enough to counter the might of an empire. Gandhi won his battle but the war between the small hands and big machines has not ended yet. Similarly, the conflict between those who believe that the earth is bequeathed to them for unchecked exploitation and those who believe that they can but enjoy their day here and then gently pass without hurting Mother Earth, is yet being played out on the canvas of history.

It is necessary to ask this question: Does the earth belong to us, or do we belong to it? John Ruskin raised this question differently when he wrote about the man sinking to the bottom of the sea with all his gold. Both Ruskin and Gandhi point to greed as the central flaw of modern technological civilisation. And in our own time, Ruskin's question acquires an even greater urgency, since an era of limitless greed legitimised as enterprise is unleashed upon us.

Such legitimised limitless greed will obviously create networks of projects, states, canons, norms, life-styles and value-structures which will correspondingly legitimise limitless harm to our planet. There is already an alarming degree of depletion of ecological resources, cultural diversity, biological versatility, and a general sense of despondency about the direction that technological civilisation has taken over the last two centuries.

But is there an alternative? Not just a dreamy idealism but a really viable alternative that will provide a foundation for a lasting shift in our ideas of progress? Is there a way of keeping our planet safe and unravished, and yet providing for the material needs of the billions spread over the continents?

Over the last two centuries practically everything done in the name of development has produced at the same time large scale tragedy and trauma for millions. Laying of railway lines, roads and other infrastructure, so necessary for national transport and global commerce have resulted in the displacement of nearly three hundred million human beings during the twentieth century. Production of pharmaceuticals and chemicals has polluted the sources of drinking water. Building up nuclear arsenals to protect national business and ideological interests has caused the serious danger of radiation. Large scale hydrological and mining projects have created vulnerability to quakes and floods. The debate between 'development' and 'displacement', between 'globalisation' and 'traumatisation', between 'progress' and 'punishment', is a difficult debate. A blind adherence to either side is full of pitfalls.

However, it is time that we realise how intricately the entire project of technology-driven economy is bound to the present national organisation. It is a cruel irony of history that while both the communist and capitalistic societies had hoped to see the end of the state, it has survived them and has remained as a strong companion of international capital. The complex relationship between nation states and international capital, which is a strange mixture of collaboration and conflict, has made the question of development far more complicated than ever before. Today, when a person wants to say a simple prayer at meal times such as 'Give us this day our daily bread…', one can hardly avoid thinking of the World Bank, the agreements on Trade and Tariff, International

Monetary Fund, inflation rates, GDPs, National Revenue Deficits, Regional Cooperation Regimes, and a hundred other things, which in the past were never related to one's health, hygiene, education and longevity.

The questions related to the future of our planet in the overall cosmic scheme, the future of the human energy in the overall scheme of the international capital, the future of the state in the context of the decline of nations, are all very large scale questions. However, every large scale question need not have an equally large scale solution. There need not even be a single solution. Perhaps a million mutinies coming from every corner of the world, south or north, black or white, ancient or modern, may help us break the developmental deadlock, so that the human, animal, and the earth itself can coexist in harmony, ceasing to be guided by greed.

I will therefore not venture to offer a single large scale formula, but will present here a story which I have partly witnessed and partly lived through. The location of the story is the majestic capital of a medieval Indian kingdom and a tiny village inhabited by a group of indigenous people, both within fifty kilometres of each other in the western part of India.

III

The name of the medieval capital city in my story is Champaner, perhaps given to it because of the pale-golden lustre of the rock surface of the mountain on which it is situated. My friend Karan Grover came to know of it through an eminent archaeologist, Professor R. N. Mehta of the Baroda University. Professor Mehta had spent nearly three decades excavating the forgotten city of Champaner, identified each and every structure in it, whether buried underground or half-preserved in ruins, or fully preserved till his time. The city was so completely forgotten that even the inhabitants of the villages in its vicinity did not claim to know much about it, though their folklore was not without memories of that glorious past. They were not however conscious of the historical truth of what they were told as stories for children. Professor Mehta excavated the entire expanse of nearly 36 square kilometres, foot by foot, having chartered the city, drawings and descriptions, and located the evidence for his discovery in historical literature. Though his discovery brought appreciation for him in archaeological circles, neither the university community at the Baroda university, nor the citizens of Gujarat state felt excited by the tremendous monumental treasure that Professor Mehta had chanced upon.

Apart from being a Professor, Mehta was also the warden of the hall of student residence in which Karan had taken lodgings as a young student of architecture. He was fond of Karan who led the University football team. One day, Mehta put his hand on Karan's shoulder and said, 'Karan, I am going to hand over Champaner to you.' The young architect accepted this offer, not knowing that he would be spending the next thirty years of his life to fulfill the dream of an ageing academic, which was also the dream of a forgotten kingdom to be brought back to life from India's cultural amnesia.

When Karan started his professional life as an architect in Baroda, he started paying frequent visits to Champaner. He still has hundreds of photographs of the buildings there which he snapped with his modest camera. One is glad that he did so, because with every passing decade, Champaner's monuments, were vandalised.

When Karan's concern and commitment grew, he decided to take up the issue with the newly founded Heritage Trust, an NGO interested in conservation, of which he was a founder member. The Heritage Trust agreed to take up Champaner as its first and most important battle.

The Heritage Trust, of which I too am a member, met to prepare a Conservation Plan. A series of Cultural Festivals were held at the sites in Champaner in order to attract the attention of the media and the citizenry. Some of the world-class artists of India came there to perform. Prominent citizens from Baroda, and other Indian cities started visiting the site. Thousands of children started congregating in Baroda to look at the exhibitions that Karan and his team had mounted in order to give voice to the being of Champaner.

The difficulties in this work were enormous. First, the general Indian apathy to history, which has become more painful owing to a wrong dichotomy between development and conservation; then, the resistance from the local population which thought that their livelihoods might get adversely affected if Champaner becomes a 'big government project'; and finally, the wrath of the government officials who felt that a civil society contribution to the task of heritage conservation was always and necessarily made in order to expose their ineffectiveness. Besides, the question of raising the funds necessary for continuing the campaign, building it up to a point of success and involving experts with various technical skills, always worked as a constraining factor.

Karan knew, however, that he owed it to Professor Mehta, to history and to the world at large, to continue his efforts. One feels happy and proud to say that in 2004, Champaner was given the status of a World Heritage Monument. I feel happy that all this was achieved; but I know that someone else may have to pledge another thirty or more years to ensure that every monument in Champaner is conserved properly, the entire area is put under a governance regime as a protected zone, and the dignity and pride with which the medieval capital lived in its own time, are gifted back to it in our time as well.

IV

Indian society is distributed into castes and adivasi communities; there are about 1500 major and minor castes and about 600 adivasi communities. The current population of the adivasis is approximately 87 million. They have continued to live side by side with the castes throughout India's history, sometimes crossing over, occasionally clashing but generally remaining affably indifferent to each other. Traditionally, the adivasi communities had been hunter-gatherers, nomads, pastoralists, feudal war-clans, and in some cases agriculturalists. The imposition of the colonial civil, criminal and forest law, which was rooted in the sedentary norms of production and governance, caused serious disruptions in the adivasi communities and started bringing them in a continuous conflict with the state. The forms of knowledge and memory developed by the adivasis have been oral. Even though tribals could paint, and even though they had their own methods to measure and count things, they had not developed scripts to record linguistic or economic transactions. During the early nineteenth century the main Indian languages were brought into the print medium; but due to the cultural and geographic isolation of the adivasis printing technology did not reach their languages. Thus, when modern India was distributed into linguistic states, the adivasi speech communities were not taken into consideration. Not having their own language states meant not having schools, colleges and universities that use the adivasi languages as the medium of instruction. Since none of the adivasi languages became an official language of administration, there have been no employment opportunities in the domain of the adivasi languages. As a result the adivasi languages in India have started becoming extinct. The 1971 Census of India had listed about 90 adivasi languages as mother tongues, each claimed by a minimum of 10,000 persons. In the 1991 Census, this figure had dropped by 18, bringing the number to 72. In other words, in India one adivasi language perishes every year. If these languages have not evolved any scripts, except in a few solitary cases, it does not mean that they do not have any significant imaginative literature. In fact adivasi literature is a valuable cultural heritage of India. It was in such a situation that a few like minded people including myself, founded the Bhasha Trust. 'Bhasha', which means 'language' or 'voice' was founded as a research and publication centre for the documentation and study of literature in the adivasi languages. The ultimate horizon of obligations for Bhasha at the moment of its inception was to document and publish fifty bilingual volumes of adivasi literature. Little did we know at that time that beyond the horizon many new worlds were waiting for us. Within months of commencing work on the 50-volume series, many adivasi writers and scholars approached me with the idea of starting a magazine in their own language, aimed at the adivasi communities. It was suggested that this magazine could be designed to be read out rather than for individual reading. Bhasha accepted the idea. The magazine was called *Dhol* (the drum), a term that has a totemic cultural significance for the adivasis. We started using the state scripts combined with a moderate use of diacritic marks to represent these languages. The response to the magazine was tremendous. More adivasis approached Bhasha, and asked for versions of *Dhol* in their own languages. In two years time *Dhol* started appearing in ten adivasi languages of western India. When the first issue of Chaudhary language *Dhol* was released, it sold 700 copies on the first day. This was a record of sorts for a little magazine. Inspired by the success of the oral magazine, our adivasi collaborators started bringing to Bhasha manuscripts of their autobiographies, poems, essays and even anthropological studies of their communities which they wanted us to publish. Subsequently, in order to highlight the oral nature of adivasi culture, we launched a weekly radio magazine which was relayed throughout the adivasi areas of Gujarat and Maharashtra. All these initiatives together gave birth to a small but focused publishing and book distribution house, which now works under the name Samas, and is the first community-owned publishing programme for adivasis and nomadic communities of India. It is not so much a commercial venture as a cultural and literary platform for intellectual concerns and a forum for expression in the people's own languages.

Oral literature, unlike written literature, is not an exclusive verbal or lexical art. It is inevitably intermixed with song, music, dance, ritual and craft. So Bhasha was drawn to the craft of the adivasi communities, initially in western India, and subsequently to craft from all over India. This resulted in Bhasha's craft collection and craft training initiatives, further leading to the formation of an adivasi craft-cooperative under the name Tribals First. The objects one identifies as craft are not produced in adivasi communities for aesthetic pleasure alone. They are invariably an integral part of daily life. Often, such objects carry with them an imprint of the supernatural as conceived in the myth and the imagination of the adivasis. The shapes, colours and the forms of these objects reflect the transactions in the adivasi's collective unconscious. Often, one overlooks the fact that the metaphysical matrix of the adivasi thought process differs markedly from the philosophic assumptions of the dominant cultural traditions in India. Therefore, sometimes simple concepts and ideas, which look perfectly natural and secular, can provoke adivasis into reacting negatively, and even violently. Any intervention in an adivasi community is likely to have a better chance of making a lasting impact if it is preceded by a sympathetic understanding of the interior landscape of the adivasi mind. The rituals, arts and craft of the adivasis reflect the complexities of their cultural norms and thought patterns as nothing else does.

I learnt the hard way that there is a common source for the dominance of the red colour in Adivasi arts, and their utter unwillingness to donate blood even when a kinsman is in dire need of blood. This common source-idea is the supernatural belief that the domain of witchcraft is red in colour. This incidental insight came in handy when we found ourselves involved in a hematological disaster called sickle cell anaemia. Reports from the Amaravati district, inhabited by the Korku adivasis, of a large number of untimely deaths of children, and similar reports from Wynad in the south, had drawn our attention to the sickle cell phenomenon. Medical sciences maintain that a certain genetic mutation required in order to fight malarial fevers has made the Adivasis prone to the sickle cell disease. On learning about the Korku trauma, we decided to check the statistics of sickle cell anaemia in our own area. Blood-testing of the adivasis is a challenging task. So we decided to draw up mathematical models, and at the same time composed an extensive family-tree through a survey that took us over two years to complete. These models and family trees enabled us to isolate certain localities, villages and families who could provide clues for coming up with the most reliable projections. We found that nearly 34 per cent of Gujarat's adivasis have been carriers of the gene disorder, and about 3.5 per cent of the population is directly affected. This means, about 2,10,000 of Gujarat's seven million adivasis are likely to not attain the age of 30. What is even more saddening is that the available health care system has not been sensitive to the epidemic scale of the gene disorder; in most instances health care remains inaccessible. This revelation was shocking to say the least. As a result, Bhasha decided to launch its health care programme under the title Prakriti. Obviously, we did not wish to create a large hospital but rather a small and functional clinic. We also wished to train local persons as community health workers so that the patients in the crisis situation could be identified and provided with immediate relief locally, and be referred to city clinics for long term treatment.

Thus, beginning with aesthetics, we found ourselves dealing with anaesthetics. We found moreover, that the two issues were intertwined.

Specific diseases may have universal scientific definitions, but the general notion of 'illness' as distinct from 'well-being' does not have a universal grammar. In a given community illness and wellness are divided by an invisible line; introduction of new medicine keeps pushing the line, enlarging the domain of anaesthetics, that is, the management of pain, and encroaching the domain of aesthetics, which is, the management of pleasure. This in turn increases the desire for instant curbing of pain, and at the same time the longing for an instant gratification of the senses.

The distribution of pain and pleasure on the cultural spectrum is in direct correspondence to the distribution of and relationship between craft and product on the economic spectrum a given community. Often, shortages caused by the larger economic forces push a social sector from its subsistence-farming character into becoming impoverished labour providers. The acute food shortages faced by the adivasis in Kalahandi and Koraput in Orissa, and the mass migration of the adivasis to the mining districts, are not exceptional stories. Though their main occupation is agriculture, adivasis have been undernourished throughout India, and sadly enough, starvation death is no news for them. Bhasha decided to set up foodgrain banks for adivasi women to address the issue of food security. Initially, we had decided to follow the government model of foodgrain banks; but we realised that they had come to be seen by adivasi villagers as charity distribution events, and so we chose to set up the grain banks without any government contribution and entirely through local participation. We feel convinced that no effort towards reducing the sickle cell incidence was likely to succeed if it was seen in isolation from the question of forced migration and food-insecurity. Food-security and health care form for us a single concern.

Soon after the Bhasha Trust was established, it decided to institute an annual lecture series named after the legendary Dr Verrier Elwin, a long time friend of India's adivasis. For the 1998 Elwin Lecture, we chose the theme of Denotified and Nomadic Tribals. There are in India about 191 communities that were once wrongly notified as 'criminal tribes' owing to the colonial government's lack of understanding of nomadic ways of life. They were restricted by law to specific localities, prevented from moving about freely; they were put to unpaid labour and stigmatised beyond redemption. After their 'denotification' in 1952, these communities, now known as the DNTs, continued to suffer stigma, social isolation and an acute economic disadvantage. Utterly dispossessed, these landless, illiterate, hounded people have been unsuccessfully trying to shake off their identities. Their estimated population is about sixty million.

Moved by the Elwin Lecture delivered by the eminent activist Mahasweta Devi, we decided to establish the DNT-Rights Action Group. It was the first national campaign ever taken up for the cause of DNT rights. In this campaign we moved the National Human Rights Commission and various ministries of the Central Government to abolish the Habitual Offenders Act, to provide a rights protection mechanism for the DNTs

Bhasha's energetic campaign for DNT rights received an overwhelming response from the denotified communities. We had opened up a long festering wound. As a leader of that campaign I had to give very serious thought to turning the anger and frustration among the demonised, brutalised and politically vandalised DNTs into a constructive energy. In order to contain the anger, I decided to use the most ancient method of getting people angry without making them destructive, which is 'theatre'. My experience of handling the violence within the minds of these communities has left me convinced that theatre is probably the most powerful cultural means of sensitising communities about the mutual entanglement and dependence of economic, social and cultural rights of several competing and clashing social sectors. Bhasha now has its own theatre group under the name Budhan Theatre, named after Budhan, a DNT killed while in police custody. Apart from the Budhan Theatre, we have so far successfully established four annual cultural festivals in as many locations of Gujarat, one of which is Dandi –the place made sacred by Gandhi's salt-satyagraha. Adivasi and nomadic performers go to these four locations on their own and people from several states participate in thousands. These melas are now there to stay.

Ever since the adivasis were brought under the provisions of the Colonial Forest Department, their access to forest produce has been steadily diminishing. They face loss of their agricultural land due to the conflict of notions about land records between them and the administration. At the same time, most adivasis have to depend merely on rain-fed cropping. These historical legacies have forced them into chronic indebtedness. Rising costs of seeds, fertilisers, fodder and electricity, as well as the costs of educating children and getting the occasional healthcare, have multiplied the cash needs of the adivasis. Unlike caste Indians who first earn and then spend, the adivasis, by and large, like to first spend and then earn just enough to meet those expenses. As such, their need for short term borrowing has increased over the years. However, they rarely default on the repayment of loans even when no written contracts are signed. These needs and habits should have been seen as a great opportunity by the formal banking sector. However, banks are barely in existence in the remote and inaccessible adivasi villages. Credit delivery is not only pathetically poor but almost non-existent, and it invariably takes a third party intervention to make the system work. Moreover, for a majority of the adivasis, institutional banking which requires written records at every stage, is a completely alien notion. On the other hand, the procedures of a private money-lender are easily comprehended by the adivasis even when the interest rates are exorbitant.

When we noticed that the interest rates (with money lenders) ranged between 60 to 120 per cent, we felt that we needed to intervene. That is why we took up the task of forming micro-credit self-help groups (SHGs). The challenges were many: getting the adivasis to understand and recognise the formal bank institution was a challenge of some magnitude; even greater was the task of educating the bank employees on their own schemes, the micro-credit policies of NABARD and the economic concerns of an NGO such as Bhasha But the most tricky issue was the peculiar social character of the private money-lender. In the adivasi areas, the money-lenders are extremely influential. They maintain an extremely complicated and not easily terminable system of accounts with their adivasi clients, that treats, cash, land, grains and labour as inter-convertible currencies. Not surprisingly, therefore, the money-lenders teamed up against Bhasha's SHGs as soon as the adivasi farmers stopped going to them. I felt quite amazed when some of the SHG members started bringing in all new and serially numbered currency notes—to pay off the bank loans they had received barely a month ago. On enquiring, we found that the money-lenders had been distributing these notes liberally to whoever was prepared to step out of the SHG.

The unease of the money-lenders continued to increase as Bhasha's micro-finance programme cut into the private credit market. There were moments when I felt that we should get into a dialogue in order to circumvent the conflict and to introduce an ethical element in their operations. But I had a naïve hope that the formal banking system might quickly step in and grab the opportunity. The money-lenders continued to feel threatened. Their fury expressed itself in March 2002, when the Hindu money-lenders bribed, coaxed and threatened a pliable section of the adivasis into making violent attacks on the families and properties of the Muslim money-lenders. Several hundred houses were burnt down, hundreds were injured, many lost their lives, and the livelihoods of thousands of adivasis and Muslims were adversely affected.

In the essay *Kikiyario* (included in this volume), I have written an elaborate analyses of the genealogy of the adivasi riots in Gujarat and how the micro-finance intervention had come to be a component with a profound significance. At the height of the riots we felt that perhaps the money-lenders may succeed in restoring once again their stranglehold on the adivasi economy. But, we found that more adivasis started forming SHGs after the riots. Since then, for our general SHG meetings, the number of adivasis wanting to participate has kept multiplying.

Bhasha has been providing training for the management of the groups, directing them to establishing viable occupations for increased income, and enabling them to form a federation of SHGs. The new occupational avenues we have opened before the adivasis include honey cultivation, specialised gum-tree plantation, brick-making and masonry, craft training, and organic cropping.In the matter of the micro-enterprise choice, the minimum guiding principle we have followed is that a new income generating activity should not lead to the adivasi's migration to the urban centres, where neither does the urban infrastructure have space for the adivasi poor, nor does the caste-bound society have any social respect for the adivasis. Therefore, we have been focusing more on the para-agricultural or value-added agricultural activities.

Over these years, I have noticed a great hunger for learning among the adivasis. Contrary to popular impression, the adivasis do want to send their children to schools. Their aspirations are belied because primary education in the adivasi villages is burdened with its own numerous structural problems. I have noticed that given a set of dedicated teachers even in the tiniest adivasi hamlets, children shape up as potentially excellent university entrants. Therefore, at Bhasha we decided to take up a programme of helping adivasi children by establishing support schools in about eighty villages, to help those who have missed the bus altogether or those who lag behind in their school studies. The results have been excellent. When I see the children in these non-formal learning centres playing, singing, painting and reading, my faith in the future of the adivasis is strengthened. Like Wordsworth, my heart too leaps up, as I behold this 'rainbow in the sky'.

Bhasha Trust established the Adivasi Academy at Tejgadh in 1999. From 2000, we have been teaching the young men and women of the area a subject that we have named 'Tribal Studies', by which we mean 'the study and understanding of how the adivasis perceive the world.' The attempt is to make our students reflect on their own situation, motivate them, and to put them onto the great task of empowering the adivasi villages by helping them to be self-reliant. The Academy offers short-term training in micro-finance, and diploma courses in Tribal Rights, Food-Security and Development, Publication and Rural Journalism, and in Tribal Arts and Museum Studies. As a rule, we do not hold examinations. The students are required to go out in the villages and set up SHGs, food-grain banks, water banks, and promote the use of solar energy and organic farming. Based on their experience of fieldwork, the students are required to write dissertations.

The Adivasi Academy is not a place for any cutting-edge theoretical knowledge. Its function is to forge strategies to improving the lives and the economic condition of the adivasis, to build durable and sustainable assets for the community, to foster respect for their cultural heritage and to provide a forum and a space for voicing adivasi concerns in an idiom of their own.

The Academy is today managed mostly by adivasis. It has its own library and a 'Museum of Voice'. Often, I am asked if a Museum of Voice had to be made the centre piece of the Academy, and, whether cultural concerns are more important than economic issues. My answer is that for communities that are culturally marginalised and economically disadvantaged, an element of pride in their identity may come handy as a strategy to empower them. Besides, cultural diversity, too, is a nation's wealth.

For the first two years, the classes were held under a majestic Mahuda tree. Then we built a small hut. Finally, we have now a red brick structure with graceful arches, built against the backdrop of the Koraj Hill. I cannot help mentioning the Koraj Hill. It houses several rock paintings dating back to 12,000 to 15,000 years, and has at its foot relics of a historical fortification belonging to the twelfth or thirteenth century. When one stands on top of the Koraj Hill, one can see a great expanse of land spreading into Gujarat, Madhya Pradesh and Maharashtra, within which several hundred adivasi villages have been waiting for over two centuries for an intervention such as the Adivasi Academy is poised to make. Visitors come to us from all parts of India and the world. A former Chief Justice of India, Justice M.N. Venkatachaliah came to visit the Academy. When the students asked him many questions, he said, 'If a tribal boy can ask the Chief Justice of India these questions, India still has hope.' The Ambassador of Netherlands and his wife felt so delighted to be with the adivasis that they sat down with them for long hours and broke the same coarse bread with them in great delight.

In the early period of my journey, I was alone. Now we are over a hundred and fifty. My hope is that the Adivasi Academy becomes the source of a many more new journeys. Of course, the road ahead is not easy to tread. The eighty-three million adivasis and sixty million DNTs is not a small number. Their problems do not have easy and ready solutions. What we have undertaken is but an experiment in shaping an alternative model of development. It is too early to judge if it will produce what it seeks to create. Yet, I believe with the poet Shelley that one must 'Hope, till Hope creates the thing it contemplates'.

V

Champaner and Tejgadh are separated only by a small range of hills, inhabited by panthers, leopards and wild life of various kinds. The rock paintings in the cave at the back of the Tribal Academy were done by an artist twelve thousand years ago. What was the quality of his joy and excitement? What had driven him to spending several years, in a lonely cave without knowing that anybody at all in a future time was going to applaud his work? Was it primitive shamanic faith that had worked as the driving spirit? Or was it something more than that? The temples atop the Pavagadh mountain, which forms the backdrop for Champaner, too were built by some nameless architects and sculptors. What was the depth of their devotion that made them give away precious years of their lives, without any hope of royal patronage, to place rock upon rock, at a place that was removed from the eyes of the world.

What was the joy and excitement of the founders of Champaner, who built enough to put a great creative century to shame? What was the spring of innovation in the great waterways and catapults they invented? What really could have been the patient labour of Professor Mehta who toiled at excavating the great historical site with the help of a very small team of assistants, while he well knew that no praise was likely to come his way? What is that human spirit, which has no visible source of inspiration, and yet it springs forth in every generation, in every century, to make this world more beautiful, more humane?

There are moments when Karan Grover and I get together. I have often asked him, 'Karan, what is it that made you give three decades of your active life to the conservation of Champaner?' His answer is a counter question, 'What is it that made you give away all your worldly possessions and your life for the cause of the tribal communities?' I once quoted lines from William Blake, 'What immortal hand or eye gave thee thy fearful symmetry?' And another time I said to Karan, 'Orpheus knew very well that if he turned his head back to look at Eurydice following him out of the depths of Hades, she would fall dead as a rock. And yet, Orpheus could sing his songs in a voice such as only gods and angels may have.' One must sing that song of Orpheus in one's own time if the human species has to sustain the great human spirit accessible to each one us. It will be there with us, wherever one is, whoever one is.

10

Gandhi Again, and Never Again

I

The following is the entry in my diary on Independence Day of 2000.

That afternoon, I had travelled to Tejgadh with Shri Nilkanth Waghmare and his gracious wife, whom I had known as parents of one of my students during the early eighties. At Tejgadh I had inaugurated the first Dilpoma Programme of the Adivasi Academy. There was no teacher other than myself. The Adivasi Academy on that day was no more than a piece of paper on which some of my colleagues and I had drafted a Constitution. On the way back from Tejgadh, as I travelled with Shri Jaswantsinh Chauhan, a one-time socialist leader, and Dr Ajay Dandekar, we debated the viability of such a dream. Ajay felt that I was rushing into the idea of the Academy a bit prematurely; I was trying to argue the need for it. The journey was long that evening, as the road's condition had worsened due to the early monsoon showers. On returning home, I sat down to write about the day's work; but surprisingly, what came out on paper was all about Mahatma Gandhi. This is what I wrote:

> The one person whose memory the nation will not forget to invoke on every Independence Day is Mohandas Karamchand Gandhi. Rabindranath Tagore gave him the title 'Mahatma'; we, the people of India,

turned him from an affectionate, though eccentric, 'Bapu' into the perennial *Rashtrapita*, the father of a nation.Sigmund Freud has analysed the uneasy relationship that exists between fathers and sons. Harold Bloom, a literary critic, used Freudian analysis to build a theory of the anxiety that a son experiences due to the father's influence. Bloom's theory postulates that a successor or the metaphorical son feels so oppressed by the presence of the predecessor or the metaphorical father that he unconsciously decides to transmute the father's presence from his existence altogether. This anxiety about the influence results in the son's adolescent attempts to be unlike his father though all such attempts are foredoomed to fail.

Half a century in a nation's history is not a very long period. The modern Indian nation may be said to have entered its adolescence at the turn of the half-century of its independence. And, therefore, at this juncture the nation seems to be engaging itself in wiping out the very presence of the Mahatma from all walks of public life. That public morality has hit an all-time low is no longer news even to a child in India. The Mahatma advocated the principle of trusteeship in dealing with the wealth of the nation. In complete denial of that principle, the states seem to be run today as little fiefdoms distributed among political leaders of all hues. The word 'truth' which was so dear to the Mahatma exists today only as an emblematic value, to be printed under the paws of the four lions watching in terror, the decline of India.

Gandhi considered villages to be the soul of India. The bubbling blood of globalisation that races through the veins of modern India has no thought left for that soul. The father preached non-violence. The children play nothing but games of violence. In short, India seems to have stepped into adolescence with the firm determination to wipe out all traces of the father's memory.

Bloom's theory, however, proposes that the metaphoric son soon realises that in the attempt to go against his father, he has in fact become his own father. Is it likely, that somewhere in this national decline there are signs of a moral resurgence? Is it possible that our reading of contemporary Indian history is completely erroneous and that the times we are passing through in fact herald times of glory?

Optimists will point out how one determined Election Commissioner could discipline erring politicians, how an alert judiciary can put the fear of law into the minds of irresponsible officials, and how a solitary civil servant can, here and there, expose the corruption of the state. These are but solitary instances. The argument in favour of contemporary India cannot be that our democracy has survived all possible subversions from within. The argument should be, on the other hand, that there is a recognition that after half a century of its survival, parliamentary democracy cannot be the ultimate system of governance in this country if we have to create a society of happy citizens. It is in this sense that we are beginning to become like Gandhi.

Gandhi was probably the most radical critic of parliamentary democracy. It has taken India half a century to be disillusioned about the desire and the ability to do good to the citizens of the country. Thanks to the electronic media, the common citizen now knows that the country is wasting huge sums on keeping the parliament functioning as a ring for bunches of hoodlums to play bullies. We have, at least, realised that Gandhi's fears about the system were not ill-founded.

The concluding sentence of *Hind Swaraj*, the youthful Gandhian utopia, rings so true today that it may be a good substitute for *satyameva jayate*. Gandhi wrote ninety years ago, 'I think we speak in the name of *swaraj*, but we have not understood its essence.' He offered a definition of *swaraj* in terms of an action plan, drawn out with his characteristic meticulousness. The Mahatma's programme has eighteen points in it. The eleventh reads, 'Let all Indians look upon the present moment as the moment for repentence, penance and bemoaning.' Most certainly, our feelings today are no different. Is it probable that out of this bemoaning will arise a new and morally reformed India?

These rhetorical questions always imply the equally rhetorical answer that at the end of every tunnel there is light, and that at the end of every night there is a dawn. Rhetoric is certainly no good for a vast sea of humanity, over a hundred crores now, and more than half of them without the means to keep their bodies and souls together. Yet, one likes to hope that since we are faced with a virtual collapse of the parliamentary system of governance, perhaps we will chalk out a new formula. Even if we make a tentative beginning in that direction at this juncture, we will have become a shade more like the Father of the Nation who, in his time and context, struggled precisely with the same problem, the problem of rescuing human dignity from the terror of power.

II

My elders often talked of the violence and bloodshed that followed the partition of India, and some of them even blamed Gandhi for the great tragedy.

I remember very clearly that Dr. Ambedkar's death was mourned by the masses with a very deep sense of bereavement.

My school teachers heatedly discussed with us the ideas of Maulana Abul Kalam Azad regarding ideal schooling for the emergent generation of children. Their eyes—I remember—lit up with dreams of a happy India.

Though my parents were not able to pay my school expenses, I could continue to study with the help of free-studentships awarded from year to year; and, in fact, though I showed no particular promise as a student at any stage, the new Indian state helped me to remain in school, college and university till I obtained a doctorate in the seventies. Those were the years when the Chinese 'agression' had pushed India into a post-Gandhian thinking about the economy and foreign policy.

The national Emergency imposed by Indira Gandhi bought the Janata Dal experiment to the centre of Indian politics. The dream of bringing freedom to the millions of Indians had already started looking like a faded painting, and a mood of despondency had already set in.

During the fifties, we used to celebrate Independence Day and Republic Day with a profound faith in the promise of the radical social transformation that was reflected in Jawaharlal Nehru's speeches and actions and the general elections. After the great split in the National Congress, the term corruption came into political discourse for the first time. 'Black money' too, began to be discussed quite openly in the newspapers. Gradually, terms like 'naxalism' and 'nepotism' started coming into the news more frequently. The main channel for the national news was still All India Radio, where Devki Nandan Pandey read out the latest in the destiny of the nation in a tone of high seriousness, and the opinion of the nation swayed in tune with the editorials of mighty journalists.

We noticed mostly through the comic eye of R.K.Laxman, that during the seventies something in the soul of India was breaking. In the international arena the term then more frequently used for India was not 'non-aligned' but 'underdeveloped'. The Bandung Conference was no longer such a thrilling memory to anybody in India. Instead, arms deals and the purchase of French fighter planes had acquired a greater urgency. The days of self-willed starvation, of rice one day every week only, associated with the stark figure of Lal Bahadur Shastri were receding, and the Green Revolution had started making the rounds in national thought.

But, of course the Green Revolution brought in some bloodshed as well. The eighties brought in violence. The Khalistan problem and the Sikh massacre, the insurgency in the Northeast, the spread of naxalism. The decade also brought into Indian consciousness the black and white Doordarshan TV channel. The nation watched with great admiration, every Sunday morning, the painstakingly slow unfolding of the *Mahabharata* and the history of Tipu Sultan's short-lived glory.

IIT graduates had by then set a good track record of finding well-paying jobs in the USA. By the middle of the seventies, the entire schooling system had been overhauled and well-tuned to producing engineers. The idealist teacher who cared for selfless work in the classroom had slowly been made to appear ridiculous. Non-school, non-collegeate tuitions had mushroomed everywhere. Electronic gadgets pouring into India though the agency of the NRIs had brought technological aid to the market place of knowledge.

The eighties, opened sluggishly, with an increase in India's borrowings. The decade in its years briefly sparkled up with Rajiv Gandhi's promise of modernisation. It ended on a note of helplessness that came in with the collapse of the USSR, India's constant ally through her hungry decades of food shortage. These years also saw an expanding engineering infrastructure.

By then the trade union movement had already given way to extortionist leadership. Therefore, when the term 'globalisation' was heard in India for the first time, people thought that it really meant 'liberalisation'. It was in this context that my thoughts first turned to the question of understanding the knowledge systems of India's adivasis.

III

I did not go to the adivasis through the writings of Verrier Elwin. I did not turn to them through any association with the Naxalites. Though Indian writing in English was becoming an academic discipline during the seventies. Elwin's name was scruplously left out of the list of writers who attracted academic attention until Arvind Krishna Mehrotra brought him in through an anthology brought out by Oxford University Press.

Though Naxalite groups emerged in many universities, and mainly in the Presidency College, Calcutta, and the Jawaharlal Nehru University, Delhi, they were primarily groups fed on a diet of heavily subsidised publications of the People's Publishing House, writing poetry and initiating dalit discontent. The Adivasi had remained remarkably quiet or unheard of in India's social discourse. There were, of course, mighty mass movements such as the Narmada Bachao Aandolan led by Medha Patkar and the Chipko forest movement of Sunderlal Bahuguna; but they appealled more to the ecological conscience of the nation, than to its understanding of the tribal and nomadic communities.

In 1984, I happened to see the statistics on Indian languages prepared by R.C.Nigam for the Indian Census of 1971. It mentioned names of languages that I had either not heard at all, or had heard and forgotten as some unessential detail. I had known that Mundari, Santhali and Bhili are large linguistic communities. The Mizo and the Bodo had been in the news for political reasons. But had I ever noted that Limbu or Korku or Dehwali too are among the languages of India? I must confess that until I started consulting the statistics of the Census, I had been woefully ignorant of the existence, of these and many other languages.

During 1985-86, Habib Tanvir came to Baroda to work with the University's Faculty of Performing Arts. Though I had numerous occasions of spending time with him, all my emotional energy was absorbed in responding to the religious hatred he had to face in Baroda. My attempts to find suitable accommodation for him met with no success. Soon after, I got involved in drought relief work. As such, the excellent opportunity of understanding something about adivasi performative traditions was lost.

It took several years before it dawned on me that because the adivasi stood on the brink of extinction, a whole continent of India's creative energy was rapidly sinking. This realisation brought into play various strands of my upbringing and sensibility. I had read in Bhalchandra Nemade's *Kosla*, a novel that I had admired with thousands of other Marathi readers, a deeply moving account of the animistic world of Dhulia's Bhilodi adivasis. I had read and published in the *Setu* magazine, which I had been editing, translations of two of Mahasweta Devi's powerful short novels. Gulam Mohammed Sheikh had introduced me to Bharat Bhawan's collection of adivasi arts. The Narmada Andolan had moved me to thinking about certain aspects of development causing silent genocides. All these, and some personal circumstances, led me to resolve that the moment to act had arrived.

IV

The adivasi of Indian has been wrapped up in two letters of the alphabet— 'ST'. Who scheduled them? When and why? Is that schedule prepared with any meaningful sociological norm to guide it? These and such other questions are rarely asked outside the classroom of anthropology. And even in these classrooms they are not asked loud and clear. It is indeed a great tragedy that the adivasis of India who number nearly ninety million do not find more than a nominal mention in the history texts of India. Their presence is almost forgotten in the social discourse; and at best they are seen as a section of India's population that is hopelessly out of step with the country's great march to modernity. Their contribution to the freedom struggle is not considered worth any mention. Their literature and arts are not considered as any expression of contemporary Indian creativity.

When I started looking at adivasi languages, the first thing I noticed was that the government was not able to do anthing for the protection or the upkeep of the languages, cultures or even of the tribes themselves. I soon noticed that a new kind of social organisation would become necessary in order to handle the challenge. I now notice that during the mid-nineties several such organisations were being established everywhere, and more so in Gujarat.

V

There is some as yet unnamed and peculiar feature of Gujarat which makes it a precursor of major shifts in the culture, economy and politics of India. Gujarat was the first to host the colonial commercial enterprise, the East India Company; the rest of India followed. Gandhi's Sabarmati Ashram came up in Gujarat, and India embraced the satyagraha model of protest. The Navanirman movement in Gujarat and the national resistance to the Emergency form one more instance. In recent years, Gujarat has provided the rest of India a model for globalised society, in terms of diasporic patterns as well as consumer splash. What precisely is the source of that collective futuristic impulse, which Gujarat punctually displays, is difficult to say.

The phenomenal growth of the non-governmental sector in the areas of social construction and empowerment area that Gujarat has witnessed over the last few decades perhaps similarly presages a major national shift in the relationship between the State and its citizens. While in most other parts of India people's organisations based on community, clan, union and professional collectivities have yet not dropped their mental habit of looking up to the government for every manner of social justice, the organisations in Gujarat have already established phenomenally successful examples of managing things without any significant support from the government. Generally known as the NGO movement, these organisations have been doing remarkable work in the area of public services and rights. One may feel uneasy with their relative tolerance towards the State's apathy and inability to protect the constitutional guarantees given to the weaker sections. Equally surprising will be found their ability to negotiate a coexistence with the corporate sector and the willingness to draw upon its practices. Both these are not NGO-like qualities.

Clearly enough, in Gujarat the sector described by the misleading title of 'NGOs' has neither a legacy of leftist social activism nor the Red Cross-Mother Teresa kind of motiveless charity. It does not fit into a set pattern. This movement is different. It articulates people's desire to build new means of self-support in the time of the demise of the State and the faceless greed of international capital. They are perhaps best described by the term 'New Social Organisations.' If one looks at the profile of NSOs in Gujarat that have won spectacular success, one will immediately realise that they cannot be classified as 'non-something', that they are not surrogates for the government, but a positive force in their own right. The most striking examples are the Ahmedabad-based SEWA, building capital for the poor, the Tribhuvandas Foundation and Sewa Rural providing healthcare, the Federation of Artisans in Kutch revitalising craft for livelihood, the Sadguru Foundation engaged in enhancing community owned water resources, and Anandi or Mahila Patchwork who work with single self supporting women. These are but a few random examples from a multitude, all of which are a cultural product of the genius of Gujarat. A careful analysis of the mission statements and the working of these organisations will reveal that they are moving in the direction of producing a model for people's organisations for a century which is likely to be far more mindless of the helpless and the deprived than all the previous centuries.

VI

Why did I think of taking up any work at all with the adivasis? Was it a romantic fascination for the unknown and the inscrutable? Was it an ideologically charged move into a social sector? Was it a purely academic project of intellectual adventure? Or was it a turning away from the tired urban social-scape?

The answer honestly, is, I do not know. It all happened to me like a current happens to a stream, restlessness to the waves and greening to a tree. If adivasis do not question how or why they do what they do, why should I?

In 1984 I had planned to set up a school in an adivasi village but I was not able to do this. In 1987-88 I took up relief work in drought-hit Savli villages, but had to give it up. In 1992, I thought I would start travelling through the adivasi villages collecting their songs and stories, but I did not. At last, in 1996, my body, mind, family and financial condition together gave me the go-ahead.

I was never alone in the work from the very beginning.

Everybody helped me. Former students from the Baroda University came as unpaid volunteers. Others started bringing in monetary contributions. Yet others came forward to adopt the ideas and execute them. Many brought new ideas. Most of all, my Adivasi Academy students! I have never ceased to learn from them.

I have not been good at inventing names and so I always choose simple words : Bhasha for the Trust, Adivasi Academy for the institute of experimental learning, *Dhol* for the magazine of tribal concerns, Vacha for the museum of voice, Samveg for the learning cottage, Vikas for the development-projects-complex, Samas for the forum of like-minded literary persons, and simply Tribals First for the first adivasi-managed tribal craft and cultural centre. I thought the fewer the words the better.

In 1996, I went to Saputara looking for tribal stories. Then some adivasis came forward to share their songs and stories. They then wanted to try their hand at the print medium. Now they write books, publish them through Bhasha, edit magazines, write plays, direct and perform them, organise adivasi literary meets. They have now become a powerful movement. Our time together has been short, but their waiting in the past had been long. They decided to speak. Bhasha facilitated this adivasi voice.

Though every day of the last seven years has been a new learning experience, the days have not been all joy and excitement. When one works with the adivasis one just cannot escape the pain and misery surrounding their existence. There is, for instance, the incurable genetic mutation causing sickle cell anaemia; the land alienation due to the stringent Forest Act; the forced migration to the construction labour market since employment opportunities as well as agricultural irrigation are not sufficiently available; and, above all, the plight of the nomads mistakenly branded as criminals, a moving story of a grave social injustice.

Had Bhasha not turned its attention to these issues we would have suffered from a sense of ethical inadequacy. A purely academic study of an adivasi language or a merely aesthetic appreciation of adivasi art may have been attempted in the past; but in our time, if these interests do not go firmly together with the concern for economic empowerment and the protection of human rights, the project is a deeply flawed one. Bhasha decided to weld together aesthetic and socio-economic concerns. May that be seen in the long term as Bhasha's positive contribution by the rest of the world. The adivasis themselves have come to realise the need for a comprehensive approach to their life and future, and have come to recognise Bhasha as their friend.

The trust that the adivasis have put in Bhasha is phenomenal. The Gram Vikas Kendras in seven locations are now working with nearly 210 villages, bringing to them microcredit self-help groups, foodgrain banks, water harvesting cooperatives, non-formal schools, craft training and healthcare. All this work is managed by adivasi men and women trained at the Tribal Academy of Tejgadh. They know that development does not mean becoming clones of the urban population. They have decided to become self-reliant. In their hearts, the days of subsidy and of a mere subsistence agricultural economy are over. The pride in their own ability to handle their developmental concerns that the adivasis working with the Gram Vikas Kendras have is the kind of new energy that will inspire them to create new ideas and imaginative expression. Real life concerns cross over into aesthetics in Bhasha, as in all truly great aesthetic experiments.

When I started the work, I did not know from where the funds would come. Our ideas were somewhat unusual and we did not know how to market them smartly. Somehow, and quite often miraculously, funding support kept coming to us, though never in tune with the requirements and never with any regularity. The precarious existence of Bhasha has now been a habit for everybody associated with it. However, for such ventures and experiments, this is but as expected.

VII

Throughout the years of my work with the adivasis, the question of social change through violence comes up again and again. The exasperation among the adivasis is so much, and the system is so utterly insensitive that any superficial thinking is bound to deduce that violence alone is the path for adivasi dignity. One day, in 2003, as I was addressing a group of young adivasi *karyakartas*, at Panvad, I decided to scribble down a set of aims for our work. They were done in Gujarati, but after returning to Baroda, I decided to have them recorded in English. Here is what I wrote:

The Ideals of Action

> Work, so that every family will have a dwelling which has windows for letting out the smoke from the kitchen, a corner or a room for children to study and keep their belongings, that men have a place of privacy to enjoy their rest, that women have spaces for keeping their clothes and carrying out the activities related to their bodies in privacy, that there are places for social gatherings, for keeping domestic animals and their young ones, for planting medicinal plants and trees for shade.
>
> Work, so that every person has the possibility of earning a livelihood, and learning new skills while carrying out the duties of his/her profession and occupation.
>
> Work, so that every person has food to eat without causing starvation of humans and slaughter of animals.
>
> Work, so that all have the clothing that they need.
>
> Work, so that everyone can travel if necessary, and can avoid travelling if it is not absolutely necessary.
>
> Work, so that there is time after work to engage in the activities of imagination, creations of the mind such as literature, the arts, music, dance, painting, photography.
>
> Work, so that there is time and desire to communicate and share the pains and pleasures of life between one human being and another.
>
> Work, so that the grandeur and beauty of the universe are not damaged and destroyed by human beings who are only one among Creation and by no means the culmination of the process of Creation.

Work, so that labour is not seen with stigma, that it has the dignity it deserves.

Work, so that a society without greed is created and stabilised, not through correction but through understanding, enlightenment and gentle persuasion.

Work, so that the mind is seen as an expression of the divine will without making that divine a dogma used for hatred and destruction.

Work, so that human thought is freed from the unnecessary fetters of nationalism, sectarian pride, racial prejudice and linguistic chauvinism.

Work, so that everybody can rise above the self-imposed divisive assertions of caste, class, creed, language, nation, race.

How beautiful life will be if all think that all deserve respect, love, care and the right to survive, if human beings allow other animals to live, without having to face a cruel extermination.

How beautiful life will be if there are no wars, no quarrels, no violence, no hatred, no greed, no exploitation, no ill health, no starvation, no inequality.

Nations, armies, courts, banks, hospitals, newspapers, television, highways, airlines are completely unnecessary for the happiness of people, and the growth of the human mind.

Governments, parliaments, laws, constitutions, currencies, taxes are completely unnecessary for the well being of human beings.

The roots of all these institutions that you think are sacred or valuable are in greed and falsehood.

Work so that they weaken and perish. Work so that one human society close to nature, close to truth, creative in imagination and strong in memory becomes possible.

The work must begin with oneself. Preaching is the worst of human faults; to be influenced by another person's preaching and to follow it blindly is the second-worst fault.

All work, thought, joy in life must always begin with oneself in order that the work, the thought, the joy are of lasting significance.

Therefore, the beginning of work is in *aparigraha,* the desire to give up the instinct to possess. Dispossess yourself, and you will know what freedom is.

Struggle for freedom from any social, historical or political structure outside the human consciousness is a struggle for shift from the slavery of one form to the slavery of another form. The one and only freedom is the freedom within one, the freedom from greed.

Economic equality imposed from outside has always led to violence and injustice. To achieve such equality has neither been possible nor been desirable. Such imposed equality has struck at the roots of creativity and innovation.

Therefore the sense of equality originating in the individual consciousness alone can help human beings to find freedom from greed. If all follow *aparigraha* as an ideal of action, all can attain *samata.*

Samata is total freedom, total justice and total equality. It is not detachment; it is different from detachment. Detachment can result in a lack of concern for pain and suffering, for violence and injustice, for slavery and the material needs of life. *Samata,* on the other hand will allow one to look upon all possessions as accidents in the economic history of a person, family or community; but at the same time it will urge one to look at suffering and pain as a cause for concern.

Aparigraha in itself is a negative instinct. If one says that one is not interested in gains, it will either be a lie or a reflection of some inadequacy. But combined with *samata, aparigraha* becomes a dynamic quality. When one says that I have made so many gains in life, how can I keep all of them to myself alone and for the gratification of my sensory pleasures alone, one becomes prepared to open up to the suffering and want that someone else also has these gains. *Samata* allows *aparigraha* to become a practical and meaningful way of life. It allows freedom to rule the instinct for greed which is also the root cause of violence.

This note has remained with me. It works as a constant reminder to me that not the more extrovert moral action of 'changing' the society as proposed in the youthful *Hind Swaraj,* but the more deepened inward-looking prayer of the Mahatma offered at the Birla House during the last fortnight of his life, is the more essential part of his being. After fifty years of my walking indifferent of him, if not entirely away from him, have I come back to him again, as Harold Bloom and Sigmund Freud had predicted for all of us ? If so, the world still has a future, which is in its great past!